P9-DFO-353

META-ANALYSIS

THE PHILIP MORRIS COLLECTION

established by the
Virginia Foundation for Independent Colleges

IN DEEP APPRECIATION
FOR THE GENEROUS SUPPORT
OF ITS MEMBER INSTITUTIONS

by

Philip Morris Companies Inc.

Studying Organizations:
Innovations in Methodology

PROJECT ON INNOVATIONS IN METHODOLOGY
FOR STUDYING ORGANIZATIONS

Project Planning Committee

Thomas J. Bouchard, *University of Minnesota*
Joel T. Campbell, *Educational Testing Service*
David L. DeVries, *Center for Creative Leadership*
J. Richard Hackman (Chair), *Yale University*
Joseph L. Moses, *American Telephone and Telegraph Company*
Barry M. Staw, *University of California, Berkeley*
Victor H. Vroom, *Yale University*
Karl E. Weick, *Cornell University*

Project Sponsorship and Administration

The volumes in this series (listed above) are among the products of a multi-year project on innovations in methodology for organizational research, sponsored by Division 14 (Industrial and Organizational Psychology) of the American Psychological Association.

Support for the project was provided jointly by the Organizational Effectiveness Research Program of the Office of Naval Research (Bert T. King, Scientific Officer), and by the School Management and Organizational Studies Unit of the National Institute of Education (Fritz Mulhauser, Scientific Officer). The central office of the American Psychological Association contributed its services for the management of project finances.

Technical and administrative support for the project was provided by the Center for Creative Leadership (Greensboro, NC) under the direction of David L. DeVries and Ann M. Morrison.

META-ANALYSIS
CUMULATING RESEARCH FINDINGS ACROSS STUDIES

by
John E. Hunter, Frank L. Schmidt,
and **Gregg B. Jackson**

Published in cooperation with Division 14 of the
AMERICAN PSYCHOLOGICAL ASSOCIATION

SAGE PUBLICATIONS
Beverly Hills / London / New Delhi

176pp

99895

Copyright © 1982 by Sage Publications, Inc.

All rights reserved. No part of this book may be reproduced or utilized in any form or by any means, electronic or mechanical, including photo-copying, recording, or by any information storage and retrieval system, without permission in writing from the publisher.

For information address:

SAGE Publications, Inc.
275 South Beverly Drive
Beverly Hills, California 90212

SAGE Publications India Pvt. Ltd.
C-236 Defence Colony
New Delhi 110 024, India

SAGE Publications Ltd
28 Banner Street
London EC1Y 8QE, England

Printed in the United States of America

Library of Congress Cataloging in Publication Data

Hunter, John.
  Meta-analysis : cumulating research findings
across studies.

  (Studying organizations : innovations in
methodology ; v. 4)
  "Published in cooperation with Division 14
of the American Psychological Association."
  Bibliography: p.
  1. Organizational research—Statistical methods.
2. Psychological research—Statistical methods.
3. Organizational behavior—Research—Statistical
methods. I. Schmidt, Frank L. II. Jackson,
Gregg B. III. American Psychological Association.
Division of Industrial-Organizational Psychology.
IV. Title. V. Series: Studying organizations ;
v. 4.
HD30.4.H86   1982   001.4'2   82-10741
ISBN 0-8039-1863-1
ISBN 0-8039-1864-X (pbk.)

FIFTH PRINTING, 1987

Contents

Preface

J. Richard Hackman

There has been increasing interest in recent years, both in academia and in society at large, in how—and how well—organizations function. Educational, human service, political, and work organizations all have come under close scrutiny by those who manage them, those who work in them, and those who are served by them.

The questions that have been raised are important ones. How, for example, can organizations become leaner (and, in many cases, smaller) as the birthrate and the rate of economic growth decline? Is there a trade-off between organizational productivity and the quality of life at work? Or can life at work and productivity be simultaneously improved? What changes in organizational practices are required to increase the career mobility of traditionally disadvantaged groups in society? How are we to understand the apparent asynchrony between the goals of educational organizations and the requirements of work organizations? How can public services be provided more responsively and with greater cost effectiveness? What new and nondiscriminatory devices can be developed to test, assess, and place people in schools and in industry? The list goes on, and it is long.

Unfortunately, there is reason for concern about our capability to build a systematic base of knowledge that can be used to deal with questions such as these. Available strategies for studying organizations have emerged more or less independently from a variety of disciplines, ranging from anthropology, sociology, and political science to educational, industrial, and organizational psychology. But none of these disciplines appears to be on the verge of generating the kind of knowledge about organizations that will be required to understand them in their full richness and complexity.

Why not? Part of the problem may have to do with the *restrictiveness* of discipline-based research—that is, the tendency of academic disciplines to support specific and focused research paradigms, and to foster intense but narrow study of particular and well-defined research "topics." Another possibility, however, is that the *methodologies* used in research on organizations have been far too limited and conventional.

In general, the methods used in studying organizations have been imported from one or another of the academic disciplines. And while these methods may be fully appropriate for the particular research problems and paradigms that are dominant in the disciplines from which they come, they also may blind those who use them to potentially significant new findings and insights about how organizations operate.

Because the need for higher quality organizational research is pressing, now may be the time to try to break through the constraints of traditional methodologies and seek new approaches to organizational research. This was the thinking of the Executive Committee of Division 14 (Industrial and Organizational Psychology) of the American Psychological Association when, a few years ago, it initiated a project intended to foster innovations in methodology for organizational research. A planning committee was appointed, and support was obtained from the Office of Naval Research and the National Institute of Education. Eighteen scholars were recruited from a variety of disciplines and formed into six working groups to review the state of organizational research methodologies, and to seek innovative approaches to understanding organizations. A three-day conference was held at the Center for Creative Leadership, at which about sixty organizational researchers (representing a variety of disciplinary orientations, and from applied as well as academic settings) reviewed the findings and proposals of the six working groups. The working groups then revised their materials based on the reactions of conference participants, and the six monographs in this series are the result.

The content of the six monographs is wide ranging, from new quantitative techniques for analyzing data to alternative ways of gathering and using qualitative data about organizations. From "judgment calls" in designing research on organizations, to ways of doing research that encourage the *implementation* of the research findings. From innovative ways of formulating research questions about organizations to new strategies for cumulating research findings across studies.

This monograph focuses specifically on innovative ways of cumulating evidence—both within single research studies and across studies of the same phenomena done at different times by different researchers. The inadequacies of traditional procedures for summarizing and making sense of findings from multiple studies are pointed out, and some new procedures for cumulating evidence using meta-analysis of research findings are presented, explained, and illustrated.

The aspiration of the numerous people who contributed their time and talent to the innovations project (they are listed facing the title page) is that readers of this monograph—and of its companions in the series—will discover here some ideas about methods that can be used to benefit both the quality and the usefulness of their own research on organizations.

—*J. Richard Hackman*
Series Editor

Introduction

☐ Scientists have known for centuries that a single study will not resolve a major issue. Indeed, a small sample study will not even resolve a minor issue. Thus, the foundation of science is the cumulation of knowledge from the results of many studies.

There are two steps to the cumulation of knowledge: (1) the cumulation of results across studies to establish facts and (2) the formation of theories to place the facts into a coherent and useful form. The focus of this book is the first of these, the resolution of the basic facts from a set of studies that all bear on the same relationship. For many years this was not an important issue in the social sciences since there was rarely more than one study dealing with a given issue. But that time has now past. There are now hundreds of studies that have sought to measure the extent to which we can predict job performance in clerical work from cognitive ability, hundreds of studies that seek to measure the effect of psychotherapy, and so on.

With as many as one hundred studies on a relationship, one might think that there would be a resolution on the issue. Yet most review studies do not conclude with resolution but with a call for more research on the question. This has been especially frustrating to organizations that fund research in the behavioral and social sciences. Many such organizations are now questioning the usefulness of research in the social sciences on just this ground. If research never resolves issues, then why spend millions of dollars on research?

In this book, we will review all the methods that have been proposed for cumulating knowledge across studies including the narrative review, counting statistically significant findings, and the averaging of quantitative outcome measures. Our critique will show that the narrative review has broken down in many cases (see also Jackson, 1978). We will note how significance counting can be done correctly (see also Rosenthal, 1978; Hedges & Olkin, 1980) in those limited conditions in which it is appropriate. Most of the book will be devoted to methods of averaging results across studies (as advocated by Glass, 1976, and Schmidt & Hunter, 1977). We will refer to the averaging methods as "meta-analysis" (we view the Glass procedure as only one such method). Most methods of meta-analysis have been concerned with one artifactual source of variation across studies: sampling error. Following the lead of work in personnel selection on "validity generalization," we will extend meta-analysis to consider two other major problems that create artifactual variation across studies: error of measurement and range variation (restriction of range in personnel selection).

The main focus of the book will be on methods of distinguishing between variance across studies due to artifacts (such as sampling error, error of measurement, and restriction in range) and variance across studies due to real moderator variables. We will also present a historical review of cumulation methods after the state-of-the-art methods have been described.

1

Integrating Research Findings Across Studies

☐ Before we delve into an abstract discussion of methods, we would like to consider a concrete example. The next section presents a set of studies to be reviewed, then a sample narrative review, followed by a critique of this review. It has been our experience that personal experience with the problems of such a review greatly quickens the learning process.

GENERAL PROBLEM AND AN EXAMPLE

A major task in all areas of science is the development of theory. In many cases, the theorists have available the results of a number of previous studies on the subject of interest. Their first task is to find out what empirical relationships have been revealed in these studies so they can take them into account in theory construction. In developing an understanding of these relationships, it is often helpful in reviewing the studies to make up a table summarizing the findings of these studies. Table 1.1 shows such a summary table put together by a psychologist attempting to develop a theory of the relationship between job satisfaction and organizational commitment. In addition to the observed correlations and their sample sizes, he has recorded data on (1) sex, (2) organization size, (3) job level, (4) race, (5) age, and

(6) geographical location. He believes variables 1, 2, 3, and 4 may affect the extent to which job satisfaction gets translated into organizational commitment. He has no hypotheses about variables 5 and 6, but has recorded them since they were often available.

As an exercise in integrating findings across studies and constructing theory, we would like for you to spend a few minutes examining and interpreting the data in Table 1.1. We would like for you to jot down the following:

(1) the tentative conclusions you reached about the relationship between job satisfaction and organizational commitment and the variables that do and do not moderate that relation; and
(2) an outline of your resulting theory of this relationship.

A TYPICAL INTERPRETATION OF THE EXAMPLE DATA

The typical report on the findings shown in Table 1.1 would run like this: The correlation between occupational commitment and job satisfaction varies from study to study with a median value of .34 and a range of -.10 to .56. Although 19 out of 30 studies found a significant correlation, 11 of 30 studies found no relationship between commitment and satisfaction. Why are commitment and satisfaction correlated within some organizations and not within others?

Table 1.2 presents a breakdown of the findings according to the features of the organization and according to the nature of the work population being studied. For example, among male work populations, commitment and satisfaction were correlated in eight studies and not correlated in seven (i.e., correlated in 53 percent of the studies), while for women there was a correlation in eleven of fifteen cases (or in 73 percent of the studies). Correlation was found in 83 percent of the large organizations, but in only 50 percent of the small organizations. Correlation was found in 79 percent of the blue-collar populations, but in only 50 percent of

TABLE 1.1 Correlations Between Organizational Commitment
and Job Satisfaction

Study	N	r	Sex	Size of Organization	White vs. Blue Collar	Race	Under vs. Over 30	North vs. South
(1)	20	.46*	F	S	WC	B	U	N
(2)	72	.32**	M	L	BC	Mixed	Mixed	N
(3)	29	.10	M	L	WC	W	O	N
(4)	30	.45**	M	L	WC	W	Mixed	N
(5)	71	.18	F	L	BC	W	O	N
(6)	62	.45**	F	S	BC	W	U	N
(7)	25	.56**	M	S	BC	Mixed	U	S
(8)	46	.41**	F	L	WC	W	Mixed	S
(9)	22	.55**	F	S	WC	B	U	N
(10)	69	.44**	F	S	BC	W	U	N
(11)	67	.34**	M	L	BC	W	Mixed	N
(12)	58	.33**	M	S	BC	W	U	N
(13)	23	.14	M	S	WC	B	O	S
(14)	20	.36	M	S	WC	W	Mixed	N
(15)	28	.54**	F	L	WC	W	Mixed	S
(16)	30	.22	M	S	BC	W	Mixed	S
(17)	69	.31**	F	L	BC	W	Mixed	N
(18)	59	.43**	F	L	BC	W	Mixed	N
(19)	19	.52*	M	S	BC	W	Mixed	S
(20)	44	−.10	M	S	WC	W	O	N
(21)	60	.44**	F	L	BC	Mixed	Mixed	N
(22)	23	.50**	F	S	WC	W	Mixed	S
(23)	19	−.02	M	S	WC	B	O	S
(24)	55	.32**	M	L	WC	W	Mixed	Unknown
(25)	19	.19	F	S	WC	B	O	N
(26)	26	.53**	F	S	BC	B	U	S
(27)	58	.30*	M	L	WC	W	Mixed	S
(28)	25	.26	M	S	WC	W	U	S
(29)	28	.09	F	S	BC	W	O	N
(30)	26	.31	F	S	WC	Mixed	U	S

*p < .05.
**p < .01.

the white-collar populations. Correlation was found in 67 percent
of the populations that were all white or mixed race, while
correlation was found in only 50 percent of those work
populations that were all black. Correlation was found in 83
percent of the cases in which the work force was all under 30 or a
mixture of younger and older workers, while not a single study
with only older workers found a significant correlation. Finally,
65 percent of the studies done in the North found a correlation,
while only 58 percent of the southern studies found a correlation.

TABLE 1.2 The Existence of Correlation Between Organizational Commitment and Job Satisfaction as Under Various Conditions Shown by the Studies in Table 1.1

Sex

	M	F	
Significant	8	11	19
Not Significant	7	4	11
	15	15	30

$$\chi^2 = 1.29$$

Organization Size

	S	L	
Significant	9	10	19
Not Significant	9	2	11
	18	12	30

$$\chi^2 = 3.44$$

Job Level

	WC	BC	
Significant	8	11	19
Not Significant	8	3	11
	16	14	30

$$\chi^2 = 2.62$$

Race

	W	B	Mix	
Significant	13	3	3	9
Not Significant	7	3	1	11
	20	6	4	30

$$\chi^2 = 1.64$$

Age

	Young	Old	Mix	
Significant	7	0	12	19
Not Significant	2	7	2	11
	9	7	14	30

$$\chi^2 = 16.52$$

Geographical Location

	North	South	
Significant	11	7	18
Not Significant	6	5	11
	17	12	29

$$\chi^2 = .12$$

Each of the differences between work populations could be regarded as the basis for a hypothesis that there is an interaction between that characteristic and occupational commitment in the determination of job satisfaction. However, some caution must be urged since the only chi-square value that is significant in Table 1.2 is that for age. That is, the difference in the frequency of

TABLE 1.3 Analysis of Correlations from Studies Based on
Younger or Mixed Age Subjects

	Sex		
	M	F	
Not Significant	3	1	4
Significant	8	11	19
	11	12	23

$\chi^2 = 1.43$

	Organization Size		
	S	L	
Not Significant	4	0	4
Significant	9	10	19
	13	10	23

$\chi^2 = 3.72$

	Job Level		
	WC	BC	
Not Significant	3	1	4
Significant	8	11	19
	11	12	23

$\chi^2 = 1.43$

	Race			
	W	B	Mix	
Not Significant	3	0	1	4
Significant	13	3	3	19
	16	3	4	23

$\chi^2 = .81$; df = 2

	Geographic Area		
	N	S	
Not Significant	1	3	4
Significant	11	7	18
	12	10	22

$\chi^2 = 1.72$

correlation between older and younger workers is significant ($\chi^2 = 16.52$; df = 2; $p < .01$), while the other differences can only be regarded as trends.

If the studies done on older workers are removed, then significant correlation is found for 19 of the remaining 23 studies. If these 23 cases are examined for relationship to organizational characteristics, then all of the chi squares are nonsignificant. These results are shown in Table 1.3. However, the chi square for size of organization is very close ($\chi^2 = 3.72$; 3.84 required). Within

TABLE 1.4   Analysis of Correlations from Studies Based on Younger and Mixed Age Subjects in Small Organizations

	Sex				Job Level		
	M	F			WC	BC	
Not Significant	3	1	4	Not Significant	3	1	4
Significant	3	6	9	Significant	3	6	9
	6	7	13		6	7	13
	$\chi^2 = 1.93$				$\chi^2 = 1.93$		

	Race					Geographical Location		
	W	B	Mix			North	South	
Not Significant	3	0	1	4	Not Significant	1	3	4
Significant	5	3	1	9	Significant	4	4	8
	8	3	2	13		5	7	12
	$\chi^2 = 1.84$					$\chi^2 = .69$		

the 23 studies with younger or mixed-age work populations, all 10 correlations for large organizations were significant.

There are thirteen studies of younger or mixed-age work populations in small organizations. None of the chi-square values even approaches signficance on this set of studies, though with thirteen cases the power of the chi-square test is low. These results are shown in Table 1.4. Within this group of studies, there is a tendency for correlation between occupational commitment and job satisfaction to be more likely to be found among women, among blue-collar workers, in all black work populations, and in the North.

Conclusion

Organizational commitment and job satisfaction are correlated in some organizational settings but not in others. In work groups in which all workers are over thirty, the correlation between commitment and satisfaction was never significant. In young or mixed-age work populations, commitment and satisfaction are always correlated in large organizations. For younger or mixed-age work populations in small organizations, correlation was found in nine of thirteen studies with no organizational feature capable of perfectly accounting for those cases in which correlation was not found.

These findings are consistent with a model that assumes that organizational commitment grows over about a ten-year period to a maximum value at which it asymptotes. Among older workers, organizational commitment may be so uniformly high that there is no variation. Hence among older workers there can be no correlation between commitment and job satisfaction. The finding for large organizations suggests that growth of commitment is slower there, thus generating a greater variance among workers of different ages within the younger group.

CRITIQUE OF THE SAMPLE REVIEW

The preceding review was constructed using standard review practices that characterize nearly all current review articles not only in psychology, but in sociology, education, and the rest of the social sciences as well. Yet every conclusion in the review is false. The data were constructed by a Monte Carlo run in which the population correlation was always assumed to be .33. After a sample size was randomly chosen from a distribution centering about 40, an observed correlation was chosen using the standard normal distribution for r with mean $\rho = .33$ and variance

$$\frac{(1 - \rho^2)^2}{N - 1}$$

That is, the variation in results in Table 1.1 is entirely the result of sampling error. Each study is assumed to be done on small sample size (i.e., less than 1000), and hence will generate an observed correlation that will depart by some random amount from the population value of .33. The size of the departure depends on sample size. Note that the largest and smallest values found in Table 1.1 are all from studies with very small samples. The larger sample size studies are all found in the central part of the range, i.e., they tend to show much less of a random departure from .33.

The moderator effects appear to make sense, yet they are purely the result of chance. The values for the organizational characteristics were assigned to the studies randomly. The fact that one of the six was highly significant is due solely to capitalization on chance.

The crucial lesson to be learned from this exercise is this: "Conflicting results in the literature" may be entirely artifactual. The data in Table 1.1 were generated by using one artifact for generating false variation across studies, sampling error. There are other artifacts that are found in most sets of studies: Studies vary in terms of the quality of measurement in their scales, researchers make computational or computer errors, people make typographical errors in copying numbers from computer output or in copying numbers from handwritten tables onto manuscripts or in setting tables into print, people study variables in settings with greater or smaller ranges of individual differences, and so on. In our experience (to be cited later), most of the interactions invented to account for differences in findings in different studies are nonexistent, apparitions composed of the ectoplasm of sampling error and other artifacts.

STATISTICAL SIGNIFICANCE TESTS

In the data set given in Table 1.1, all population correlations are actually equal to .33. Of the 30 correlations, 19 were found to be statistically significant, i.e., came out in the right direction. But 11 of the 30 correlations were not significant. That is, the significance test gave the wrong answer 11 out of 30 times, an error rate of 37 percent. In oral presentation, many express shock that the error rate can be greater than 5 percent. The significance test was derived in response to the problem of sampling error, and many believe that the use of significance tests guarantees an error rate of 5 percent or less. This is just not true. Statisticians have pointed this out for many years; the possibility of high error rates is brought out in discussions of the "power" of statistical tests. However, statistics teachers are all well aware that this point is missed by most students. The 5 percent error rate is only guaranteed if the null hypothesis is true. If the null hypothesis is false, then the error rate can go up to 95 percent.

Let us state this in more formal language. If the null hypothesis is true for the population and our sample data leads us to reject it, then we have made a Type I error. If the null hypothesis is false for the population and our sample data leads us to accept it, then we have made a Type II error. The statistical significance test is defined in such a way that the Type I error rate is at most 5 percent. However the Type II error rate is left free to be as high as 95 percent. The question is which error rate applies in a given study. The answer is that the relevant error rate can only be known if we know whether the null hypothesis is true or false for that study. If we know that the null hypothesis is true, then we know that the significance test has an error rate of 5 percent. Of course, if we know that the null hypothesis is true and we still do a significance test, then we should be told to wear a dunce cap. If we know the null hypothesis to be true, then we can obtain a 0 percent error rate by ignoring the data. That is, there is a fundamental circularity to the significance test. If you do not know whether the null hypothesis is true or false, then you do not know whether the error rate is the Type I error rate or the Type II; i.e., you do not know if your error rate is 5 percent or some value as high as 95 percent. There is only one way to guarantee a 5 percent error rate in all cases: abandon the significance test and use a confidence interval.

Consider our hypothetical example from Table 1.1. But let us simplify the example still further by assuming that the sample size is the same for all studies, say $N = 40$. The one-tailed significance test for a correlation coefficient is $\sqrt{N-1}\ r \geqslant 1.64$; in our case

$\sqrt{39}\,r \geqslant 1.64$ or $r \geqslant .26$. If the population correlation is .33 and the sample size is 40, the mean of the sample correlations is .33, while the standard deviation is $(1 - \rho^2)/\sqrt{N-1} = (1 - .33^2)/\sqrt{39} = .14$. Thus, the probability that the observed correlation will be significant is the probability that the sample correlation will be greater than .26 when it has a mean of .33 and a standard deviation of .14.

$$P\left\{r \geqslant .26\right\} = P\left\{\frac{r - .33}{.14} \geqslant \frac{.26 - .33}{.14}\right\} = P\left\{z \geqslant -.50\right\} = .69$$

That is, if all studies were done with a sample size of 40, then a population correlation of .33 would mean an error rate of 31 percent.

Suppose that we alter the population correlation in our hypothetical example from .33 to .20. Then the probability that the observed correlation will be significant drops from .69 to

$$P\left\{r \geqslant .26\right\} = P\left\{z \geqslant \frac{.26 - .20}{.15} = .39\right\} = .35$$

That is, the error rate rises from 31 percent to 65 percent. In this realistic example, we see that the error rate can be over 50 percent. A two to one majority of the studies can find the correlation to be not significant despite the fact that the population correlation is always .20.

Error rates of over 50 percent have been shown to be the usual case in personnel selection research. Thus reviewers who count the number of significant findings are prone to incorrectly conclude that a given procedure does not predict job performance. Furthermore, as Hedges and Olkin (1980) point out, this situation will only get worse as more studies are done. The reviewer will become ever more convinced that the majority of studies show no effect and that the effect thus does not exist.

If the null hypothesis were true in a set of studies, then the base rate for significance is not 50 percent but 5 percent. If more than one in twenty studies finds significance, then the null hypothesis must be false in some studies. We must then avoid an error made by some of the reviewers who know the 5 percent base rate. Given 35 percent significant findings, some have concluded that "Since 5 percent will be significant by chance, this means that the number of studies in which the null hypothesis is truly false is 35 - 5 = 30 percent." Our hypothetical example shows this reasoning to be false. If the population correlation is .20 and the sample size is 40, then there will be signficiant findings on only 35 percent of the studies even though the null hypothesis is false in all cases.

The typical use of significance test results leads to terrible errors in review studies. Most review studies falsely conclude that further research is needed to resolve the "conflicting results" in the literature. These errors in review studies can only be eliminated if errors in the interpretation of significance tests can be eliminated. Yet those of us who have been teaching power to generation after generation of graduate students have been unable to change the reasoning processes and the false belief in the 5 percent error rate. If there is an alternative analysis, then maybe it is time to abandon the significance test.

There are two alternatives to the significance test. At the level of review studies, there is meta-analysis. At the level of single studies, there is the confidence interval.

THE CONFIDENCE INTERVAL

Consider studies 17 and 30 from our hypothetical example in Table 1.1. Study 17, with r = .31 and N = 69, finds the correlation to be significant at the .01 level. Study 30, with r = .31 and N = 26, finds the correlation to be not significant. That is, two authors with identical finding, r = .31, come to opposite conclusions. Author 17 concludes that organizational commitment is highly related to job satisfaction, while Author 30 concludes that they are independent. Thus two studies with identical findings can lead to a review author claiming "conflicting results in the literature."

The conclusions are quite different if the results are interpreted with confidence intervals. Author 17 reports a finding of r = .31

with a 95 percent confidence interval of $.10 \leqslant \rho \leqslant .52$. Author 30 reports a findings of r = .31 with a 95 percent confidence interval of $-.04 \leqslant \rho \leqslant .66$. There is no conflict between these results. On the other hand, the fact recorded by the significance test is still given in the two confidence intervals. Study 17 finds the $\rho = 0$ is not a reasonable possibility, while study 30 finds that $\rho = 0$ cannot be ruled out. Thus the two separate studies do not draw conclusions inconsistent with the significance test. But the two studies considered together lead to the correct conclusion if confidence intervals are used.

Consider now studies 26 and 30 from Table 1.1. Study 26 finds r = .53 with N = 26, which is significant at the .01 level. Study 30 finds r = .31 with N = 26, which is not significant. That is, we have two studies with the same sample size but apparently widely divergent results. Using significance tests, one would conclude that there must be some moderator that accounts for the difference. This conclusion is false.

Had the two studies used confidence intervals, the conclusion would be different. The confidence interval for study 26 is $.25 \leqslant \rho \leqslant .81$ and the confidence interval for study 30 is $-.04 \leqslant \rho \leqslant .66$. It is true that the confidence interval for study 30 includes $\rho = 0$, while the confidence interval for study 26 does not; this is the fact registered by the significance test. But the crucial thing is that the two confidence intervals show an overlap of $.25 \leqslant \rho \leqslant .66$. Thus consideration of the two studies together leads to the correct conclusion that it is possible that both studies could imply the same value for the population correlation ρ. Indeed the overlapping intervals include the correct value $\rho = .33$.

Two studies with the same population value can have nonoverlapping confidence intervals, but this is a low probability event (about 5 percent). But then confidence intervals are not the optimal method for looking at results across studies; that distinction belongs to meta-analysis.

Confidence intervals work better than significance tests for two reasons: First, the interval is correctly centered on the observed value rather than on the hypothetical value of the null hypothesis. Second, it gives the author a correct image of the extent of uncertainty in small-sample studies. It may be disconcerting to see a confidence interval as wide as $-.04 \leqslant \rho \leqslant .66$, but that is far superior to the frustration produced over the years by the false belief in "conflicting results."

Confidence intervals enable us to define the phrase "small sample size." Suppose that we want the confidence interval for the correlation coefficient to define the correlation to the first digit, i.e., to have a width of $\pm .05$. Then for small population correlations, the minimum sample size is 1538. In order that a sample size of 1000 be sufficient, the population correlation must be at least .44. Thus, for correlational studies, "small sample size" includes all studies with less than a thousand persons and often extends higher yet.

There is a similar calculation for those who cumulate across experimental studies. If the cumulating statistic is to be the d statistic (by far the most frequent choice at this time), then small effect sizes will be specified to their first digit only if the sample size is 3076. If the effect size is greater than 0, then the sample size must be even greater than 3076. If the difference between the population means is .3 standard deviations or more, then the minimum sample size to yield d to within $\pm .05$ of .30 is 6216. Thus, for experimental studies, "small sample size" begins with 3000 and often extends well beyond that.

Confidence intervals give a correct picture of the extent of uncertainty that surrounds results computed from small-sample studies. However, the only way to eliminate uncertainty is to either run large-sample, single studies or to combine results across many small-sample studies. Given the limited resources available to social scientists, this means that the only answer open in most areas is meta-analysis.

META-ANALYSIS

Is there a quantitative analysis that would have suggested that all the differences in Table 1.1 might stem from sampling error?

Suppose we compute the variance of the correlations, weighting each by its sample size. The value we obtain is .02258 (SD = .150). We can also compute the variance expected solely on the basis of sampling error. The formula for the sampling error variance of each individual correlation r_i is $(1 - .331^2)^2/(N_i - 1)$, where .331 is the sample size weighted mean of the correlations in Table 1.1. If we weight each of these estimates by its sample size (as we did in the case of the observed variance), the formula for variance expected from sampling error is:

$$S_e^2 = \frac{\sum\limits_{i=1}^{i=30} \left[\frac{N_i(1 - .331^2)^2}{N_i - 1} \right]}{\sum N_i}$$

This value is .02058 (SD = .144). The ratio of variance expected from sampling error to actual (observed) variance is .02058/.02258 = .91. Thus sampling error alone accounts for an estimated 91 percent of the observed variance in the correlations. The best conclusion is that the relation between job satisfaction and organizational commitment is constant across sexes, races, job levels, age, geographical locations, and size of organization. The best estimate of this observed value is .331—the sample size weighted mean of the thirty correlations. Our analysis indicates this relation holds across ages, sexes, races, geographical locations, job levels, and different sized organizations. When people in oral presentations analyzed the data from these thirty studies qualitatively, different people came to different conclusions. In contrast, all researchers applying the quantitative method used here would (barring arithmetic errors) come to exactly the same conclusion.

For theoretical purposes, the value .331 is not the one we want, since it has been attenuated by unreliability in both measures. Suppose from information in the thirty studies, we estimate the average reliability of job satisfaction measures at .70 and the average reliability of organizational commitment measures at .60.

Then the correlation between true scores on each measure is
$.331/\sqrt{.70(.60)} = .51$.

In many research areas the complexity of the task of integrating
findings across studies in a qualitative manner is much greater
than the task presented by the data in Table 1.1—because the
number of studies to be integrated is much greater than thirty.
Traditional review procedures are inadequate to integrate
conflicting findings across large numbers of studies. As Glass
(1976, p. 4) has pointed out, the results of hundreds of studies "can
no more be grasped in our traditional narrative discursive review
than one can grasp the sense of 500 test scores without the aid of
techniques for organizing, depicting and interpreting data." In
such areas as the effects of class size on student learning, the
relation of IQ to creativity, and the effects of psychotherapy on
patients, literally hundreds of studies can accumulate over a period
of only a few years. Glass (1976) has noted that such studies
collectively contain much more information than we have been
able to extract from them to date. He points out that because we
have not exploited these gold mines of information, "We know
much less than we have proven." What is needed are methods that
will integrate results from existing studies to reveal patterns of
relatively invariant underlying relations and causalities, the
establishment of which will constitute general principles and
cumulative knowledge. Such methods would allow not only
theoretical advances, but important contributions to the solution
of applied problems in society. To date, social science studies
conducted to provide policy guidance—for example, on the
question of busing to attain racial balance in the schools—have
produced conflicting findings. If this continues to be the case,
government and society may become increasingly disenchanted
with psychology and the social sciences, feeling that every new
study on any social issue or problem will only produce different
and conflicting results.

At one time in the history of psychology and the social sciences,
the pressing need was for more empirical studies examining the
problem in question. In many areas of research, the need today is
not additional empirical data but some means of making sense of

the vast amounts of data that have accumulated. Given the increasing number of areas within psychology and the other social sciences in which the number of available studies is quite large and the importance to theory development and practical problem solving of integrating conflicting findings to establish general knowledge, it is likely that methods for doing this will attain increasing importance in the future. Such methods can be built around statistical procedures that are already familiar to us. As Glass (1976, p. 6) has stated:

> Most of us were trained to analyze complex relationships among variables in the primary analysis of research data. But at the higher level, where variance, nonuniformity and uncertainty are no less evident, we too often substitute literary exposition for quantitative rigor. The proper integration of research requires the same statistical methods that are applied in primary data analysis.

ORGANIZATION OF THE BOOK

In normal science writing, historical review is presented first. However, in our case, the historical review is very difficult for novices to read. In effect, the new methods can only be compared to earlier methods if the new methods are first understood. Therefore, we will first present state-of-the-art meta-analysis. Then we will present our review and critique of earlier methods.

In the course of doing a meta-analysis, the steps would be (1) search for and gather studies, (2) extract information from the studies, (3) cumulate the information extracted. We will talk about all three steps, but not in their natural chronological order. The reason for this is that in order to know what is good or bad procedure in early steps, you must know what you are going to do in the last step. Thus, we will cover meta-analysis first, then return to issues of defining the study domain, deciding what to code, and writing up the review report. Finally, we will go back one step further by making a long list of recommendations for changes in publication practices necessary for optimal cumulation of results across studies.

2

Cumulation Procedures
An Overview and
Some Problems

WHEN AND HOW TO CUMULATE

Cumulation of results across studies is conceptually a simple process:

(1) calculate the desired descriptive statistic for each study available, and average that statistic across studies,
(2) calculate the variance of the statistic across studies,
(3) correct the variance by subtracting the amount due to sampling error,
(4) correct the mean and variance for study artifacts other than sampling error, and
(5) compare the corrected standard deviation to the mean to assess the size of the potential variation in results across studies in qualitative terms. If the mean is more than two standard deviations larger than 0, then it is reasonable to conclude that the relationship considered is always positive.

In practice, cumulation can run into a variety of technical side issues that we will take up in later sections: cumulation of multiple results within studies and transformation of published results into the desired descriptive statistic. If the corrected variation across studies is large, then there are the problems of capitalization on chance that accompany the search for moderator variables.

Cumulation of results can be used whenever there are at least two studies with data bearing on the same relation. For example, if your study at Crooked Corn Flakes contains a correlation between job status and job satisfaction, then you might want to compare that correlation with the correlation found in your earlier study at Tuffy Bolts. However, to correct for sampling error with two correlations, it is possible to use a strategy different from the corrected variance procedure laid out in Chapter 3. Instead, it is possible to simply test the correlations to see if they are significantly different. If they are not significantly different, then the difference between them may be due solely to sampling error. The fact that one study was done in the food industry while the other study was done in manufacturing is probably irrelevant.

Ideally, cumulation of results works best if it is based on a large number of studies acquired by exhaustive search procedures. However, cumulation is also valid for "convenience" samples of studies that just happen to lie at hand. This is particularly true if the corrected standard deviation suggests that all the variation across studies is due to sampling error. If all the variation is due to sampling error, then the accuracy of the mean value in relation to the one true population value is determined by the total number of subjects across studies. Even a relatively small number of studies may have a large cumulative sample size.

If a convenience sample of studies has a small corrected standard deviation, then there is essentially no variation in the results across the population of studies that is implicitly sampled. However, the investigator may have *systematically* excluded studies that others would have put in the same population of studies. In this case, the basis for the exclusion might be a real moderator variable and the population of excluded results might cluster around a different population value. Reliance on a convenience sample always involves some risk.

It has long been alleged that published studies have much stronger results than unpublished ones, partly because the published studies are better designed, but partly because editorial reviewers have a substantial preference for studies with statistically significant results. There may be some research areas in which the true effect size is zero. In such an area, if some studies with Type I errors get published, and most studies without Type I errors do not get published, an assessment limited to published studies would be biased. Even if the effect size is not zero, there may still be bias in the estimation of its size (although by definition there could be no Type I errors).

Two recent studies provide some evidence that unpublished studies do have smaller effect sizes. Smith and Glass (1977) analyzed the standardized effect sizes of 375 studies on psychotherapy. They found that studies published in books had an average effect size of .8σ, those published in journals had an average effect size of .7σ, dissertations averaged .6σ, and unpublished studies averaged .5σ. Rosenthal and Rubin (1978) found that in a sample of interpersonal expectancy effect studies the average effect size of 32 dissertations was .35σ and the average effect size of 313 nondissertations was .65σ. Neither set of authors reported an assessment of the relative methodological quality of the published and unpublished studies. It seems likely that most of the difference between the average effect size of the published and unpublished studies is due to differences in the methodological quality. If attenuation effects were properly corrected for, differences might disappear (see Schmidt & Hunter, 1977, p. 536-537).

UNDERCORRECTION FOR ARTIFACTS IN THE CORRECTED STANDARD DEVIATION

The corrected standard deviation of results across studies should always be regarded as an overestimate of the true standard deviation. Procedures developed to date correct for only some of the artifacts that produce spurious variation across studies. There are other artifacts that have similar effects. The largest of these is computational or reporting errors. If you have 30 correlations ranging from .00 to .60, and one correlation of −.45 (a case we encountered in our own studies), then it is virtually certain that the outlier resulted from some faulty computational or reporting procedure; for example, failing to reverse the sign of a variable that is reverse scored, or using the wrong format in a computer run, or a typographical error, and so on. Other artifacts that create spurious variation across studies include: differences in the reliability of measurement, differences in the validity of measurement (such as criterion contamination or criterion deficiency in personnel selection studies), differences in the extent of individual differences in the populations of different studies (such as differences in restriction in range in personnel selection studies), and differences in the amount of the treatment. Indeed, the relevant question in many settings will be: Is all of the variation across studies artifactual? In the personnel selection area, we have reached exactly this conclusion on a number of topics such as single-group validity, differential validity by race or ethnic group, specificity of test validity across setting or time, and amount of halo in judgments made using different methods.

Some artifacts can be quantified and corrected for. Corrections for differences in reliability and restriction in range were made by Schmidt, Hunter, Pearlman, and Shane (1979) and are given in Chapter 3. Differences in validity of measurement could be corrected using similar techniques if there is an integrated study available that provides a path analysis relating the alternate measures to each other. Quantitative differences in treatment effects (such as the percentage incentive) can be coded and corrected after the initial cumulation establishes the relation (if any) between that aspect of the treatment and study outcome.

However, these corrections depend on additional information, which is frequently not available. For example, reliabilities and standard deviations are rarely published in correlational studies. They are not even considered in most experimental studies. And alas, computational and reporting errors will never be quantified and eliminated.

If there is a large, real variation in results across studies, then any conclusion based solely on the summary result entails a certain amount of error. This is the familiar problem of ignoring interactions or moderator effects. However, errors of even greater magnitude can be made if false variation is attributed to nonexistent methodological and substantive moderators. For example, one well-known psychologist recently became so discouraged by the variation in results in several research areas that he declared that no finding in psychology would ever hold from one generation to the next since each cohort would always differ on some social dimension. This is the reification of sampling error. It leads not only to disillusionment, but also to immense wasted effort in endlessly replicating studies in which enough data already exist to resolve the issue.

If there is a large corrected standard deviation, then it may be possible to explain the variations across studies by breaking the studies into groups on the basis of the relevant difference between them. This breakdown can be an explicit subdivision of studies into categories or it can be an implicit breakdown using regression methods to correlate study outcomes with study characteristics. Both of these will be considered in detail in Chapter 3 and 4. However, we will show in the next section that such a breakdown should only be attempted if there is a large corrected variance. Otherwise the breakdown can introduce error into the interpretation of the studies by virtue of capitalization on chance.

CODING STUDY CHARACTERISTICS AND CAPITALIZATION ON CHANCE

The process of meta-analysis is defined by Glass and his associates as a composite process: (1) cumulation of descriptive statistics across studies, (2) the coding of 50 to 100 study characteristics such as date of study, number of threats to internal validity, and so forth, and (3) regression of study outcome onto the coded study characteristics. Such coding can be 99 percent of the work in the research integration process. Yet this coding work may be entirely wasted. In our own research in which we have made corrections for sampling error and other artifacts, we have found no significant remaining variation across studies. That is, it is our experience that there is usually no important variation in study results after sampling error and other artifacts are removed. Thus all observed correlations with study characteristics would be the result of sampling error and capitalization on chance due to the small number of studies.

If there is little variation other than sampling error, then correlating study characteristics with study outcome leads to massive capitalization on chance. The sample size for looking at study characteristics is not the number of persons in the studies but the number of studies. For example, the multiple regression of study outcome onto forty study characteristics (typical of current studies) with only fifty studies as observations (typical of current studies) would lead by chance to a multiple correlation near one. This is clear from standard shrinkage formulas using the number of studies as the number of observations. Indeed, some studies have more study characteristics than studies, a situation in which the multiple correlation is always 1.00 by fiat.

Many meta-analysts falsely believe they avoid this problem by the following strategy. They first look through their forty study characteristics to find the five that are most highly correlated. Then they use multiple regression with those five, using a shrinkage formula (if it is used at all) for five predictors. But to pick the best five out of forty is approximately the same as doing a step-up regression from forty predictors, and hence one should use forty in the shrinkage formula rather than five. In many cases, correct shrinkage would show the multiple correlation to be near zero.

To take all variation across studies at face value is to ignore sampling error. Since most studies are done with very small samples (i.e., less than 500 subjects), the sampling error is actually quite large in comparison to observed outcome values. Thus to ignore sampling error is to guarantee major statistical errors at some point in the analysis. The classical reviewer's error is to report the range of outcome values. The error in current meta-analyses is capitalization on chance in relating variation across studies to coded study characteristics.

We do not claim that we have the answer to the problem of capitalization on chance. It is our opinion that there is no solution to this problem within statistics. It is well known within statistics that the statistical test does not solve the problem; the Type I versus Type II error tradeoff is unavoidable. Thus if issues are to be resolved solely on statistical grounds, then the answer to subtle questions can only be to gather more data, often much more data. The other alternative is to develop theories that allow new data to be drawn indirectly into the argument. This new data may then permit an objective resolution of the issue on theoretical grounds.

The two most common empirical designs are the correlational study and the two-group intervention study. Strength of relationship in correlational designs is usually measured by the correlation coefficient. We will give formulas for cumulating the correlation coefficient in Chapter 3. Some have argued that the slope or covariance should be cumulated rather than the correlation. However, slopes and covariances are comparable across studies only if exactly the same instruments are used to measure the independent and dependent variables in each study. It is a rare set of studies in which this is true. Thus only in rare cases can the slope or covariance be cumulated because it is in the same metric in all studies. Furthermore, the strength of relationship represented by a slope or covariance can only be known when these numbers are compared to the standard deviations, i.e., only when the correlation coefficient is computed. We are leaving cumulation formulas for the slope, intercept, and covariance for the next edition.

The statistic most commonly reported in intervention studies is the t-test statistic. However, t is not a good measure of strength of effect since it is multiplied by the square root of sample size and hence does not have the same metric across studies. When sample size is removed from the t statistic, the resulting formula is the effect size statistic d. We will consider the point-biserial correlation and the effect size statistic d in Chapter 4. Some would argue for proportion of variance, but that statistic has two defects. First, it does not preserve the sign or direction of the treatment effect. Second, as a consequence of the loss of sign, the squared effect measure is biased. Cumulation formulas for proportion of variance and auxillary statistics such as the ratio of standard deviations will also be left for the next edition.

Cumulation formulas will next be developed for the two major relational statistics: the correlation coefficient and the effect size statistic used to assess interventions. Formulas for the correlation coefficient are presented in Chapter 3. Formulas for the effect size statistics are given in Chapter 4. These chapters will assume that each entry is based on a statistically independent sample. However, it frequently is possible to obtain more than one relevant estimate of a correlation or effect size from the same study. How then should multiple estimates of a relation from within the same study contribute to a cumulation across studies? This issue is taken up in Chapter 5.

3

Cumulating Correlations Across Studies

☐ The correlation coefficient is subject to three sources of error that we can eliminate at the level of meta-analysis: sampling error, error of measurement, and range variation.

At the level of the single study, sampling error is a random event. If the observed correlation is .30, then the population correlation could be higher than .30 or lower than .30 and there is no way that we can correct for it. However, at the level of meta-analysis, sampling error can be estimated and corrected for. Consider first the operation of averaging correlations across studies. When we average correlations, we also average the sampling errors. Thus the sampling error in the average correlation is the average of the sampling errors in the individual correlations. For example, if we average across 30 studies with a total sample size of 2000, then sampling error in the average correlation is about the same as if we had computed a correlation on a sample of 2000. That is, if the total sample size is large, then there is very little sampling error in the average correlation.

The variance of correlations across studies is another story. Squaring the deviations eliminates the sign of the sampling error and hence the tendency for errors to cancel themselves out in summation. Instead, sampling error causes the variance across studies to be systematically larger than the variance of population correlations that we would like to know. However, the effect of sampling error on the variance is to add a known constant, which we will call the sampling error variance. This constant can be subtracted from the observed variance. The difference is then an estimate of the desired variance of population correlations.

To eliminate the effect of sampling error from a meta-analysis, we must transform the distribution of observed correlations into a distribution of population correlations. That is, we would like to replace the mean and standard deviation of the observed sample correlations by the mean and standard deviation of population correlations. Since sampling error cancels out in the average correlation across studies, our best estimate of the mean population correlation is simply the mean of the sample correlations. However, sampling error adds to the variance of correlations across studies. Thus we must correct the observed variance by subtracting the sampling error variance. The difference is then the variance of population correlations across studies.

Once we have corrected the variance across studies for the effect of sampling error, it is possible to see if there is any real variance in results across studies. If there is a large amount of variance across studies, then it is possible to look for moderator variables to explain that variance. To test a hypothesized moderator variable, we break the set of studies into subsets using the moderator variable. For example, we might split the studies into those done on large corporations and those done on small businesses. We then do separate meta-analyses within each subset of studies. If we find large differences between subsets, then the hypothesized variable is indeed a moderator variable. The meta-analysis within subsets also tells us how much of the residual variance within subsets is due to sampling error and how much is real. That is, the meta-analysis tells us whether or not we need look for a second moderator variable.

Although it is pedagogically convenient to present the search for moderator variables immediately after presenting the method for eliminating the effects of sampling error, that search is actually premature. Sampling error is only one source of artifactual variation across studies. We should eliminate other sources of variance before we look for moderator variables.

The second largest source of variation across studies in most domains is variation in error of measurement across studies. That is, a variable such as job satisfaction can be measured in many ways. Thus different studies will often use different measures of the independent variable or different measures of the dependent variable. Alternate measures will differ in the extent to which they are affected by random error of measurement. Differences in amount of error produce differences in the size of the correlation. Differences in correlations across studies due to differences in error of measurement would look like differences due to a moderator variable. Thus we only obtain a true picture of the stability of results across studies if we eliminate the effects of measurement error.

At the level of the individual person, error of measurement is a random event. If Billy's observed score is 75, then his true score could be either greater than 75 or less than 75 and there is no way of knowing which. However, when we correlate scores across persons, the random effects of error of measurement produce a systematic effect on the correlation coefficient. Error of measurement in either variable causes the correlation to be lower than it would have been with perfect measurement. We will show a formula for "attenuation" that states the exact extent to which the correlation is lowered by any given amount of error of measurement. This same formula can be algebraically reversed to provide a formula for "correction for attenuation." That is, if we know the amount of error of measurement in each variable, then we can "correct" the observed correlation to provide an estimate of what the correlation would have been had the variables been perfectly measured.

The amount of error of measurement in a variable is measured by a number called the "reliability" of the variable. The reliability is a number between 0 and 1 that measures the percentage of the observed variance that is due to the true score. That is, if the reliability of the independent variable is .80, then 80 percent of the variance is due to the true score, and by subtraction, 20 percent of the variance is due to error of measurement. In order to correct for the effect of error of measurement on the correlation, we need to know the amount of error of measurement in both variables. That is, in order to correct the correlation for attenuation, we need to know the reliability of both variables.

Error of measurement can be eliminated from a meta-analysis in either of two ways: at the level of single studies or at the level of averages across studies. If the reliability of each variable is known in each study, then the correlation for each study can be separately corrected for attenuation. We can then do a meta-analysis on the corrected correlations. However, many studies do not report the reliability of their instruments. Thus reliability information is only sporadically available. Under such conditions we can still estimate the distribution of the reliability of both the independent and the dependent variables. Given the distribution of observed correlations, the distribution of the reliability of the independent variables, and the distribution of the reliability of the dependent variable, it is possible to derive special formulas to correct the meta-analysis to eliminate the effects of error of measurement.

If each individual correlation is corrected for attenuation, then the meta-analysis will differ slightly from the meta-analysis on uncorrected correlations. The average corrected correlation is a good estimate of the average population correlation between true scores. But the variance is again too large because of the additive nature of sampling error on variance. The observed variance can be corrected for sampling error simply by subtracting a constant—the sampling error variance. However, the sampling error in a corrected correlation is larger than the sampling error in an uncorrected correlation. Therefore, a different formula must be used to compute the sampling error variance for corrected correlations.

In many contexts, the distribution of the independent variable is approximately the same across studies. In such cases, the meta-analysis need not correct for range variation. However, if the standard deviation of the independent variable differs radically from study to study, then there will be corresponding differences in the correlation from study to study. These differences across studies will look like differences produced by a moderator variable. Thus if there are big differences in the range of the independent variable across studies, then a true picture of the stability of results will appear only if the effects of range variation are eliminated. To do this, we compute the value that the correlation would have had had the study been done on a population with some reference level of variance on the independent variable.

Range deviation can be corrected at the level of the single study. If we know the standard deviation of the independent variable in the study, and if we know the standard deviation in the reference population, then there is a range correction formula that will produce an estimate of what the correlation would have been had the standard deviation of the study population been equal to the standard deviation of the reference population. If we correct a correlation for range departure, then the corrected correlation will have a different amount of sampling error than an uncorrected correlation. Therefore, a meta-analysis on corrected correlations would use a different formula for the sampling error variance.

In an ideal research review, we would have complete information about artifacts on each study. For each study, we would know the extent of range departure and the reliabilities of both variables. We could then correct each correlation for both range departure and error of measurement. We would then do a meta-analysis of the fully corrected correlations.

Alas, most research reports do not include a table of standard deviations. Thus information on range departure is only sporadically available. However, we may be able to compile information about the distribution of range departure across studies. If we can, then there is a formula for correcting the meta-analysis to eliminate the effects of range variation.

In a research area in which studies are subject to large range departure, the typical meta-analysis will be done in three stages. First, the studies are used to compile information on four distributions: the distribution of the observed correlations, the distribution of the reliability of the independent variable, the distribution of the reliability of the dependent variable, and the distribution of range departure. That is, there would be four means and four variances compiled from the set of studies using each study to provide whatever information it has. Second, the distribution of correlations would be corrected for sampling error. Third, the distribution corrected for sampling error would then be corrected for error of measurement and range variation. This fully corrected distribution could then be examined for evidence of moderator variables. If there appears to be a moderator variable, then the data could be analyzed by subsets to test moderator candidates.

The remainder of this chapter will be presented in three main sections. First, there will be a complete treatment of meta-analysis with correction for sampling error only. Second, there will be a treatment of error of measurement and range departure written as if full information on reliability and range departure is available for each study. Third, we will present the meta-analysis methods required if only the distributions of artifacts are known.

It is important to keep in mind that even a fully corrected meta-analysis will not correct for all artifacts. Even when sampling error, error of measurement, and range variation are gone, there is still reporting error, and bad data, and departures from construct validity, and so on. That is, even after correction, variation across studies should be taken with a grain of salt. Small residual variance is probably due to uncorrected artifacts rather than to a real moderator variable.

SAMPLING ERROR

ESTIMATION

If the population correlation is assumed to be constant over studies, then the best estimate of that correlation is not the simple mean across studies but a weighted average in which each correlation is weighted by the number of persons in that study. Thus the best estimate of the population correlation is:

$$\bar{r} = \frac{\Sigma [N_i r_i]}{\Sigma N_i}$$

where r_i is the correlation in study i and N_i is the number of persons in study i. The corresponding variance across studies is not the usual sample variance, but the frequency weighted average squared error

$$s_r^2 = \frac{\Sigma [N_i (r_i - \bar{r})^2]}{\Sigma N_i}$$

Two questions are often asked about the procedure above: First, is the weighted average always better than the simple average? Second, why do we not transform the correlations to Fisher z form for the cumulative analysis? The answer in both cases is that we have found the procedure described here to be preferable.

The frequency weighted average gives greater weight to large studies than to small studies. If there is no variance in population correlations across studies, then the weighting always improves accuracy. If the variance of population correlations is small, then the weighted average is also always better. If the variance across studies is large, then as long as sample size is not correlated with the size of the population correlation, the weighted average will again be superior. That leaves one case in which the weighted average could prove troublesome. For example, we have found thirteen studies on the validity of bio-data in predicting job success. One of these studies was done by an insurance consortium with a sample size of 15,000. The other twelve studies were done with sample sizes of 500 or less. The weighted average will give the single insurance study over thirty times the weight given to any other study. In a situation such as this, we recommend two analyses: a first analysis with the large sample study included and a second analysis with the large sample study left out. We have not yet had to figure out what to do should the two analyses show a major discrepancy. (In our case, they did not.)

What about the Fisher z transformation? In our original work, we did things both ways: for preliminary calculations done by hand, we averaged correlations themselves, but on the computer we used what we thought to be the superior Fisher z transformation. For several years we noticed no difference in the results for these two analyses, but in our validity generalization study for computer programmers (Schmidt, Gast-Rosenberg, & Hunter, 1980), the difference was dramatic. The average validity using the Fisher z transformation was considerably larger (by about .07) than the average validity when correlations were averaged without this transformation. Careful checking of the mathematics then showed that it is the Fisher transformation that is biased. The Fisher z transformation gives larger weights to large correlations than to small ones. Hence the positive bias.

The fact that the Fisher z transformation leads to bias in averaging correlations does not mean that there is any problem with the transformation in the context for which it was invented, i.e., confidence intervals. The Fisher z transformation expands large correlations relative to small ones, which causes the confidence interval around large correlations to be smaller than those around small correlations. However, the confidence intervals around large correlations should be smaller because sampling error is smaller. Thus the expansion has the desired effect on confidence intervals (as was Fisher's intent in deriving the z transformation).

CORRECTING THE VARIANCE FOR
SAMPLING ERROR AND AN EXAMPLE

How much variation in correlations is there across studies? The observed variance s_r^2 is a confounding of two things: variation in population correlations (if there is any) and variation in sample correlations produced by sampling error. Thus an estimate of the variance in population correlations can be obtained only by correcting the observed variance s_r^2 for sampling error. The following mathematics shows that sampling error across studies behaves exactly like error of measurement across persons, and that the resulting formulas are exactly comparable to standard formulas in classical measurement theory (reliability theory).

Let us use an error variable e_i to represent the sampling error in the sample correlation in study i, i.e., we define e_i by

$$r_i = \rho_i + e_i$$

Then the mean of the error is

$$E(e_i) = 0$$

and its variance is denoted

$$\sigma_{e_i}^2 = \frac{(1 - \rho_i^2)^2}{N_i - 1}$$

This formula is entirely analogous to the true score, error score formula

$$X_p = T_p + e_p$$

where X_p and T_p are the observed and true scores for person p. In particular, sampling error is unrelated to population values across studies. Thus if we calculate a variance across studies, then the variance of sample correlations is the sum of the variance in population correlations and the variance due to sampling error, i.e.,

$$\sigma_r^2 = \sigma_\rho^2 + \sigma_e^2$$

Since the mean error is 0 within each study, the error variance across studies in the average within study variance

$$\sigma_e^2 = \text{ave } \sigma_{e_i}^2 = \frac{\Sigma\left[N_i\,\sigma_{e_i}^2\right]}{\Sigma N_i} = \frac{\Sigma\left[N_i\left[\dfrac{(1-\rho_i^2)^2}{N_i-1}\right]\right]}{\Sigma N_i}$$

The fraction $N_i/(N_i-1)$ is close to unity. If we take this fraction as unity, and we use the approximation that average $(\rho^2)\cong(\text{average } \rho)^2$, then we have the almost perfect approximation

$$\sigma_e^2 = \frac{(1-\bar{r}^2)^2 K}{N}$$

where K is the number of studies and $N = \Sigma N_i$ is the total sample size. Using s_r^2 as the estimate of the variance of r, we have

$$\text{est } \sigma_\rho^2 = \sigma_r^2 - \sigma_e^2 = s_r^2 - \frac{(1-\bar{r}^2)^2 K}{N}$$

An Example: Socioeconomic Status and Police Performance

Bouchard (1776, 1860, 1914, 1941) postulated that differences in upbringing would produce differences in response to power over other people. His theory was that since lower-class parents obtain obedience by beating their kids to a pulp while middle-class parents threaten them with loss of love, lower-class children would grow into adults who are more likely themselves to use physical force to gain compliance. He tested his theory by looking at the relationship between socioeconomic status and brutality in police departments. His independent measure was socio-economic status measured in terms of six classes ranging from 1 = upper, upper class to 6 = lower, lower class. His brutality measure was the number of complaints divided by the number of years employed. Only patrol officers were considered in the correlations (see Table 3.1).

TABLE 3.1 Correlations Between Socioeconomic Status and Police Brutality (U.S.)

Location	Date	Sample Size	Correlation
Philadelphia	1776	100	.34*
Richmond, VA	1861	100	.16
Washington, DC	1914	50	.12
Pearl Harbor	1941	50	.38*

*Significant at the .05 level.

$$\bar{r} = \frac{100(.34) + 100(.16) + 50(.12) + 50(.38)}{100 + 100 + 50 + 50} = \frac{75.00}{300} = .25$$

$$\sigma_r^2 = \frac{100(.34 - .25)^2 + 100(.16 - .25)^2 + 50(.12 - .25)^2 + 50(.38 - .25)^2}{100 + 100 + 50 + 50}$$

$$= \frac{3.31}{300} = .0110$$

$$\sigma_e^2 = \frac{(4)(1 - .25^2)^2}{300} = \frac{3.52}{300} = .0117$$

$$\sigma_\rho^2 = \sigma_r^2 - \sigma_e^2 = .0110 - .0117 = -.0007$$

$$\sigma_\rho = 0$$

Bouchard claimed that his results varied dramatically from city to city. His explanation was that Washington and Richmond are southern cities, and that southern hospitality is so strong that it reduces the incidence of brutality in the lower classes and hence reduces the correlation in those cities. However, our analysis shows that his variation in results is just sampling error.

A SIGNIFICANCE TEST FOR VARIATION ACROSS STUDIES

If the corrected variance across studies is positive, then it may still be trivial in size. Indeed, it may even be due to sampling error. This section presents a statistical significance test for whether the observed variation is greater than that expected by chance. However, we do not endorse this significance test because it asks the wrong question. Signficant variation may be trivial in magnitude, and even nontrivial variation may still be due to research artifacts.

If a sample correlation is drawn from a population in which the variables are approximately bivariate normal (or are dichotomous), then the sample correlation has mean:

$$E(r) = \rho$$

where ρ is the population correlation and a variance of

$$\sigma_r^2 = \frac{(1 - \rho^2)^2}{N - 1}$$

where N is the sample size for that study. For a single study, the following modified squared deviation has a chi-square distribution with 1 degree of freedom;

$$\chi_1^2 = \frac{(N - 1)}{(1 - \rho^2)^2} \ (r - \rho)^2$$

If these squared deviations are summed across studies, then the sum has a chi-square distribution with K degrees of freedom, where K is the number of studies:

$$\chi_K^2 = \sum_i \frac{N_i - 1}{(1 - \rho_i^2)^2} (r_i - \rho_i)^2$$

Under the null hypothesis that all population correlations are equal, i.e., under the assumption that $\rho_i = \rho$ for all i, the best estimate of them is $\bar{r}$, the weighted average sample correlation, i.e.,

$$E(\bar{r}) = \rho$$

and the modified deviation statistic using $\bar{r}$ for ρ has a chi-square distribution with $K - 1$ degrees of freedom.

$$\chi^2_{K-1} = \Sigma \frac{(N_i - 1)(r_i - \bar{r})^2}{(1 - \bar{r}^2)^2}$$

To a close approximation, this is equal to:

$$\chi^2_{K-1} = \frac{1}{(1 - \bar{r}^2)^2} \Sigma N_i (r_i - \bar{r})^2$$

If we now multiply through by unity in the form of N/N, where $N = \Sigma N_i$ is the total number of persons across studies, we get

$$\chi^2_{K-1} = \frac{N}{(1 - \bar{r}^2)^2} s_r^2$$

This statistic can be used for a formal test of no variation, though it has very high statistical power and will therefore reject the null hypothesis given a trivial amount of variation across studies. Thus if the chi square is not signficant, this is strong evidence that there is no true variation across studies; but if it is significant, the variation may still be negligible in magnitude.

MODERATOR VARIABLES ANALYZED
BY GROUPING THE DATA

A moderator variable is a variable that causes differences in the correlation between two other variables. For example, in the police study above, Bouchard postulated that geographic region (North versus South) would be a moderator variable for the relationship between socioeconomic status and brutality. If there is true variation in results across studies, then there must be such a moderator variable (or possibly more than one) to account for such variance. On the other hand, if the analysis shows that the variation in results is due to sampling error, then any apparent moderating effect is due to capitalization on chance. This was the case in Bouchard's work.

If the correction for sampling error indicates a substantial variation in population correlations across studies, then any potential moderator variable can be used to group the observed correlations into subsets. Within each subset, we can calculate a mean, a variance, and a variance corrected for sampling error. A moderator variable will show itself in two ways: (1) the average correlation will vary from subset to subset and (2) the corrected variance will average lower in the subsets than for the data as a whole. These two facts are not mathematically independent. By a theorem in analysis of variance, we know that the total variance is the mean of the subset variances plus the variance of the subset means. Thus the mean uncorrected within subset variance must decrease to exactly the extent that the subset means differ from one another.

An Example: Police Brutality in Transylvania

In order to justify a European sabbatical, Hackman (1978) argued that Bouchard's work on police brutality needed a cross-cultural replication. So he gathered data in four cities in Transylvania, carefully replicating Bouchard's measurement of socioeconomic status and brutality. His data is given along with Bouchard's in Table 3.2.

Analysis of the Whole Set

$$\bar{r} = \frac{100(.34) + \ldots + 100(.19) + \ldots + 50(.23)}{100 + \ldots + 100 + \ldots + 50} = \frac{105.00}{600} = .175$$

$$\sigma_r^2 = \frac{100(.34 - .175)^2 + \ldots + 50(.23 - .175)^2}{100 + \ldots + 50} = \frac{9.995}{600} = .0167$$

$$\sigma_e^2 = \frac{(1 - .175^2)^2 8}{600} = .0125$$

$$\sigma_\rho^2 = .0167 - .0125 = .0042$$

$$\sigma_\rho = .065$$

TABLE 3.2   Correlations Between Socioeconomic Status
and Police Brutality (U.S. and Transylvania)

Investigator	Location	Sample Size	Correlation
Bouchard	Philadelphia	100	.34*
Bouchard	Richmond, VA	100	.16
Bouchard	Washington, DC	50	.12
Bouchard	Pearl Harbor	50	.38*
Hackman	Brasov	100	.19
Hackman	Targul-ocna	100	.01
Hackman	Hunedoara	50	−.03
Hackman	Lupeni	50	.23

*Significant at the .05 level.

The corrected standard deviation of .065 is enough smaller than
the mean of .175 that the qualitative nature of the relationship is
clear; the population correlation is positive in all studies. However, the variation is not trivial in amount.

America	Transylvania
$\bar{r} = .25$	$\bar{r} = .10$
$\sigma_r^2 = .0110$	$\sigma_r^2 = .0110$
$\sigma_e^2 = .0117$	$\sigma_e^2 = .0133$
$\sigma_\rho^2 - -.0007$	$v_\rho^2 - -.0023$
$\sigma_\rho = 0$	$\sigma_\rho = 0$

Analysis of the subsets shows a substantial difference in mean
correlations, $\bar{r} = .25$ in America and $\bar{r} = .10$ in Transylvania. The
corrected standard deviations reveal that there is no variation
in results within countries.

Hackman explained the difference between the two countries
by noting that vampires in America live quiet contented lives
working for the Red Cross, while vampires in Transylvania must
still get their blood by tracking down and killing live victims.
Vampires in Transylvania resent their low station in life and
focus their efforts on people of high status whom they envy.

Middle-class policemen who work at night are particularly vulnerable. Thus, there is less variation in social class among the policemen in Transylvania and this restriction in range reduces the correlation.

After a heated exchange at the Academy of Management convention, Bouchard bared his fangs and showed Hackman that American vampires can still be a pain in the neck. Bouchard then noted that the difference in the results reflected the fact that his studies were done at times when the country was going to war. This increase in aggressive excitement raised the general level of brutality and thus increased its reliability of measurement and hence the level of correlation. Hackman made no reply.

According to both Bouchard's and Hackman's explanations, the underlying relation between brutality and socioeconomic status is actually the same in both countries. That is, the regression equation and amount of error about the regression line are predicted to be identical. For example, according to Bouchard's theory, higher brutality variance in America produces the higher correlation. This hypothesis could be tested by doing a cumulative analysis of the standard deviations. Slopes and intercepts could also be cumulated.

CORRECTING FEATURE CORRELATIONS FOR SAMPLING ERROR

Suppose that some feature of study i is coded as a quantitative variable y_i. Then that feature can be correlated with the outcome statistic across studies. For example, if correlations between dependency and school achievement varied as a function of the age of the child, then we might code average age in study i as y_i. We could then correlate age of children with size of correlation across studies. An example of this method is given by Schwab, Olian-Gottlieb, and Heneman (1979). However, such a correlation across studies is a confounding of the correlation for population values with y and the noncorrelation of the sampling error with y. This is directly analogous to the role of error of measurement in attenuating correlations based on imperfectly measured variables. Thus the observed correlation across studies will be smaller than would be the case had there been no sampling error.

To avoid confusion between the basic statistic r, which is the correlation over persons within a study, and correlations between r and study features over studies, the correlations over studies will be denoted by the symbol "Cor." For example, the correlation between the correlation r and the study feature y across studies will be denoted Cor (r,y). This is the observed correlation across studies, but the desired correlation across studies is that for population correlations ρ_i, i.e., the desired correlation across studies is Cor (ρ, y). Starting from the formula $r_i = \rho_i + e_i$, we calculate a covariance over studies and use additivity of covariances to produce

$$\sigma_{ry} = \sigma_{\rho y} + \sigma_{ey} = \sigma_{\rho y} + 0 = \sigma_{\rho y}$$

If this covariance across studies is divided by standard deviations across studies, then we have

$$Cor(r,y) = \frac{\sigma_{ry}}{\sigma_r \sigma_y} = \frac{\sigma_{\rho y}}{\sigma_r \sigma_y}$$

$$= \frac{\sigma_{\rho y}}{\sigma_\rho \sigma_y} \frac{\sigma_\rho}{\sigma_r}$$

$$= Cor(\rho,y) \frac{\sigma_\rho}{\sigma_r}$$

But the covariance of r_i with ρ_i is

$$\sigma_{r\rho} = \sigma_{\rho\rho} + \sigma_{e\rho} = \sigma_{\rho\rho} + 0 = \sigma_\rho^2$$

and hence, the correlation across studies is

$$Cor(r,\rho) = \frac{\sigma_{r\rho}}{\sigma_r \sigma_\rho} = \frac{\sigma_\rho^2}{\sigma_r \sigma_\rho} = \frac{\sigma_\rho}{\sigma_r}$$

Thus the observed correlation across studies is the product of two other correlations, the desired correlation and reliability-like correlation.

$$Cor(r,y) = Cor(\rho,y) \, Cor(r,\rho)$$

The desired correlation is then the ratio

$$Cor(\rho,y) = \frac{Cor(r,y)}{Cor(r,\rho)}$$

which is precisely the formula for correction for attenuation due to error of measurement if there is error in one variable only. What is the correlation between r and ρ over studies? We have the variance of r as estimated by s_r^2. We need only the variance of ρ, which was estimated in the previous section of this chapter. Thus the "reliability" needed for use in the attenuation formula is given by

$$\text{Reliability of r} = \left\{Cor(r,\rho)\right\}^2$$

$$= \frac{\sigma_\rho^2}{\sigma_r^2} = \frac{s_r^2 - K(1 - \bar{r}^2)^2/N}{s_r^2}$$

An Example: The Tibetan Employment Service

Officials in the Tibetan Employment Service have been using a cognitive ability test for some years to steer people into various jobs. Although they have relied on content validity for such assignments, they have also been gathering criterion-related validity data to test their content validity system. In their content validity system, test development analysts rate each occupation for the extent to which it requires high cognitive ability, with rating from 1 = low to 3 = high. They have concurrent validity

TABLE 3.3 Tibetan Employment Service Content Validity Test

Occupation	Rating	Validity (Correlation)	Sample Size
Monastery Abbot	3	.45*	100
Magistrate	3	.55*	100
Holy Man	2	.05	100
Farmer	2	.55*	100
Bandit	1	.10	100
Yak Chip Collector	1	.10	100

*Significant at the .05 level.

studies on six occupations chosen to stratify the full range of the content validity continuum (see Table 3.3).

$$\bar{r} = .30$$

$$\sigma_r^2 = .0483$$

$$\sigma_e^2 = .0083$$

$$\sigma_\rho^2 = .0483 - .0083 = .0400$$

$$\sigma_\rho = .20$$

$$Rel(r) = \frac{\sigma_\rho^2}{\sigma_r^2} = \frac{.0400}{.0483} = .83$$

Let y_i be the cognitive rating of the ith occupation. Then

$$Cor(r,y) = .72$$

$$Cor(\rho,y) = \frac{.72}{\sqrt{.83}} = .79$$

The study found very large variation in validity even after correction for sampling error. The correlation was .72 between rating and observed correlation, and rose to .79 after correction for sampling error.

ARTIFACTS OTHER THAN SAMPLING ERROR

ERROR OF MEASUREMENT AND
CORRECTION FOR ATTENUATION

Variables in science are never perfectly measured. Indeed, sometimes the measurement is very rough. Since the turn of the century we have known that the effect of error of measurement is to attenuate the correlation coefficient. That is, error of measurement systematically lowers the correlation between variables. This systematic error is then exaggerated by the unsystematic distortions of sampling error. In this section we will review the theory of error measurement and derive the classic formula for correction for attentuation. We will then look at the impact of error of measurement on sampling error and confidence intervals. In particular, we will derive the confidence interval for corrected correlations. From this base we will later consider the impact of error of measurement as it varies in amount from one study to another.

Let us denote by T the true score that would have been observed on the independent variable had we been able to measure it perfectly. We then have

$$x = T + E_1$$

where E_1 is the error of measurement in the independent variable. Let us denote by U the true score that would have been observed on the dependent variable had we been able to measure it perfectly. We then have

$$y = U + E_2$$

where E_2 is the error of measurement in the dependent variable. Let us use the traditional abuse of notation by denoting the reliabilities by r_{xx} and r_{yy}, respectively. We then have

$$r_{xx} = \rho_{xT}^2$$

$$r_{yy} = \rho_{yU}^2$$

The desired correlation is the population correlation between perfectly measured variables ρ_{TU}, but the observed correlation is the sample correlation between observed scores r_{xy}. There are then two steps in relating the one to the other: the systematic attenuation of the population correlation by error of measurement and the unsystematic variation produced by sampling error.

The systematic attenuation can be computed by considering the causal pathways from x to T to U to y:

$$\rho_{xy} = \rho_{xT}\rho_{TU}\rho_{Uy} = \rho_{xT}\rho_{yU}\rho_{TU}$$

$$= \sqrt{r_{xx}}\ \sqrt{r_{yy}}\rho_{TU}$$

At the level of population correlations, this leads to the classic formula for correction for attenuation

$$\rho_{TU} = \frac{\rho_{xy}}{\sqrt{r_{xx}}\ \sqrt{r_{yy}}}$$

At the level of observed correlations, we have

$$r_{xy} = \rho_{xy} + e$$

where e is the sampling error in r_{xy} as before. Thus

$$\sigma_r^2 = \sigma_\rho^2 + \sigma_e^2$$

where the error variance is given by the formulas of earlier sections.

If we correct the observed correlation using the population correlation formula, then we have the following equation:

$$r_c = \frac{r_{xy}}{\sqrt{r_{xx}}\ \sqrt{r_{yy}}} = \frac{\sqrt{r_{xx}}\ \sqrt{r_{yy}}\ \rho_{TU} + e}{\sqrt{r_{xx}}\ \sqrt{r_{yy}}}$$

$$= \rho_{TU} + \frac{e}{\sqrt{r_{xx}}\ \sqrt{r_{yy}}}$$

We can write a new equation for the corrected correlation

$$r_c = \rho_c + e_c$$

where e_c is the sampling error in the corrected correlation r_c, and where the population value $\rho_c = \rho_{TU}$. The error variance for the corrected correlation can then be computed from the error variance for uncorrected correlations and the reliabilities of the two variables.

$$e_c = \frac{e}{\sqrt{r_{xx}} \sqrt{r_{yy}}}$$

$$\sigma_{e_c}^2 = \frac{\sigma_e^2}{r_{xx} r_{yy}}$$

Thus if we correct the observed correlation for attenuation, we increase the sampling error correspondingly. In particular, to form the confidence interval for a corrected correlation, we apply the correction formula to the two endpoints of the confidence interval for the uncorrected correlation. That is, in the case of correction for attenuation, just as we divide the point estimate of the correlation by the product of the square roots of the reliabilities, so too we divide each endpoint of the confidence interval by the same product.

An Example of Correction for Attenuation

Suppose that if organization commitment and job satisfaction were perfectly measured, then the correlation between true scores would be $\rho_{TU} = .60$. Suppose instead that we measure organization commitment with reliability $r_{xx} = .45$ and that we measure job satisfaction with reliability $r_{yy} = .55$. Then the population correlation between observed scores would be

$$\rho_{xy} = \sqrt{r_{xx}} \sqrt{r_{yy}} \rho_{TU} = \sqrt{.45} \sqrt{.55} (.60) = .30$$

That is, the effect of error of measurement in this example is to reduce the correlation between true scores of .60 to a correlation of .30 between observed scores. If we apply the correction formula we have

$$\rho_{TU} = \frac{\rho_{xy}}{\sqrt{r_{xx}}\ \sqrt{r_{yy}}} = \frac{.30}{\sqrt{.45}\ \sqrt{.55}} = \frac{.30}{.50} = .60$$

That is, correction for attenuation works perfectly for population correlations.

Consider the impact of sampling error. If the sample size for the study is $N = 100$, then the standard deviation of the observed correlation (from $\rho_{xy} = .30$) is $(1 - .30^2)/\sqrt{99} = .091$. Thus it would not be uncommon to observe a correlation of .20 in the actual study. If we compare the observed correlation of .20 to the desired correlation .60, then we see that there is a massive error. However this error can be broken into two components; the systematic error of attenuation and the unsystematic error due to sampling error. The systematic error reduced the correlation from .60 to .30. The unsystematic error is shown in the comparison of .20 to the population attenuated correlation .30.

Let us correct for attenuation and look at the error in the corrected correlation.

$$r_c = \frac{r_{xy}}{\sqrt{r_{xx}}\ \sqrt{r_{yy}}} = \frac{.20}{\sqrt{.45}\ \sqrt{.55}} = \frac{.20}{.50} = .40$$

The sampling error in the corrected correlation is the difference between the estimated .40 and the actual .60. Thus we have

$$r = \rho + e = \rho - .1$$

$$r_c = \rho_c + e_c = \rho_c - .2$$

So as we doubled the observed attenuated correlation in order to estimate the unattenuated correlation, so we doubled the sampling error as well. On the other hand, we reduced the systematic error from .30 to 0.

The standard error for the observed correlation is

$$\frac{1 - .20^2}{\sqrt{99}} = .096$$

The confidence interval for the observed correlation is given by r $\pm$ 1.96 σ_e = .20 $\pm$ 1.96 (.096) or .01 $\leqslant \rho \leqslant$ .39, which does include the actual value of ρ_{xy} = .30. We then correct each endpoint of the confidence interval to obtain

Lower Endpoint	Upper Endpoint
$r_1 = .01$	$r_2 = .39$
$r_{1c} = \dfrac{.01}{\sqrt{.45}\ \sqrt{.55}}$	$r_{2c} = \dfrac{.39}{\sqrt{.45}\ \sqrt{.55}}$
$= \dfrac{.01}{.50} = .02$	$= \dfrac{.39}{.50} = .78$

Let us compare the confidence intervals of corrected and uncorrected correlations:

$$.01 \leqslant \rho_{xy} \leqslant .39$$

$$.02 \leqslant \rho_{TU} \leqslant .78$$

We see that the center of the confidence interval changes from the uncorrected correlation .20 to the corrected correlation .40. At the same time, the width of the confidence interval doubles, reflecting the increased sampling error in the corrected correlation.

This point can be made dramatically with confidence intervals. If a correlation is near .60, then the sampling error will be near $(1 - .60^2)/\sqrt{99} = .064$. This is much smaller than the sampling error near a correlation of .30, which is .091. Thus if we can eliminate error of measurement substantively, then we obtain larger observed correlations with *smaller* confidence intervals. Substantive elimination of error of measurement is vastly superior to elimination by statistical formula after the fact.

We could have obtained the same result in a different way. Suppose that we erected the confidence interval around the corrected correlation using the sampling error formula for e_c. The center of the confidence interval is then $r_c = .40$. The sampling error is than given by

$$\sigma^2_{e_c} = \frac{\sigma^2_e}{r_{xx} r_{yy}} = \frac{\sigma^2_e}{(.45)(.55)} = \frac{(1 - .2^2)^2/99}{.2475} = .0376$$

That is, the sampling error in the corrected correlation is $\sigma_{e_c} = .19$. The confidence interval is then given by $.40 \pm 1.96 \, \sigma$ or $.02 \leqslant \rho_{TU} \leqslant .78$.

STATISTICAL VERSUS SUBSTANTIVE CORRECTION

If we use statistical formulas to correct for attenuation, then we obtain larger corrected correlations with a wider confidence interval. There are two conclusions that might be drawn from this fact. *False conclusion:* Since correcting for attenuation increases the amount of sampling error, maybe we should not correct for attenuation. *Key fact:* If we do not correct for attenuation, then we do not reduce the *systematic* error. In our example, the error in the uncorrected correlation was $.60 - .20 = .40$. Thus the error in the corrected correlation was only half as great as the error in the uncorrected correlation. *True conclusion:* We could greatly improve our statistical accuracy if we could eliminate the error of measurement substantively, i.e., by using better measurement procedures in the first place.

RESTRICTION OR ENHANCEMENT OF RANGE

If studies differ greatly in the range of values present on the independent variable, then the correlation will differ correspondingly. Thus correlations are only directly comparable across studies if they are computed on population with the same standard deviation on the independent variable. There is a range correction formula that will take a correlation computed on a population with a given standard deviation and produce an estimate of what the correlation would have been had the standard deviation been different. That is, the range correction formula estimates the effect of changing the study population standard deviation from one value to another. To eliminate range variation from a meta-analysis, we can use the range correction formula to project all correlations to the same reference standard deviation. For each study we need to know the standard deviation of the independent variable s_i. Range departure is then measured by relating that standard deviation to the reference standard deviation S. The comparison used is the ratio of the standard deviation in the study group to the reference standard deviation, i.e., $u = s/S$. The ratio u is less than 1 if the study has restriction in range. The ratio u is greater than 1 if the study has enhancement of range. The correlation in the study will be greater than or less than the reference correlation depending on whether the ratio u is greater than or less than 1, respectively.

In this section, we will consider range departure in the context of a single study in which population correlations are known. In the following section we will consider the effect of correcting a sample correlation for range departure. We will find that the sampling error of the corrected correlation differs from that of the uncorrected correlation, and we will show how to adjust the confidence interval correspondingly. We will then briefly note the relation between the ratio u and the "selection ratio" in personnel selection research. After this treatment of range correction in single studies, we will consider the effect of range correction in meta-analysis.

We cannot always study the population that we wish to use as a reference point. Sometimes we study a population in which our independent variable varies less than in the reference population (restriction in range) and sometimes we study a population in which it varies more widely than in the reference population (enhancement of range). In either case, the same relationship between the variables produces a different correlation coefficient. In the case of restriction in range, the study population correlation is systematically smaller than in the reference population. In the case of enhancement of range, the study population correlation is systematically bigger than the reference population correlation. This problem is compounded by sampling error and by error of measurement.

Consider personnel selection research. The reference population is the applicant population, but the study is done with people who have already been hired (since we cannot get job performance scores except for those who get to work). If the people hired were a random sample of the applicants, then our only problem would be sampling error. But suppose that the test we are to use for prediction has been used to select those who are hired. For example, suppose that those hired are those who are above the median on the test. Then the range of test scores among the job incumbents is greatly reduced in comparison to the applicant population. We would thus expect a considerable reduction in the size of the population correlation that we wish to estimate. If test scores are normally distributed in the applicant population, then the standard deviation for people in the top half of the distribution is only 60 percent as large as the standard deviation for the entire population. Thus if the standard deviation were 20 in the applicant population, it would be only .60(20) = 12 in the incumbent population of those hired. The degree of restriction in range would thus be u = 12/20 = .60.

The formula for the correlation produced by a change in distribution in the independent variable is called the formula for restriction in range, although it works for enhancement too as we shall see. Let ρ_1 be the reference population correlation and let ρ_2 be the study population correlation. Then

$$\rho_2 = \frac{u\rho_1}{\sqrt{(u^2 - 1)\rho_1^2 + 1}}$$

where

$$u = \frac{\sigma_{x_2}}{\sigma_{x_1}}$$

is the ratio of standard deviations in the two populations. In the case of restriction in range, we have $u < 1$ and hence $\rho_2 < \rho_1$. In the case of range enhancement, we have $u > 1$ and hence $\rho_2 > \rho_1$.

In the case of our personnel selection example, we have $u = .60$ and hence

$$\rho_2 = \frac{.60\rho_1}{\sqrt{(.60^2 - 1)\rho_1^2 + 1}} = \frac{.60\rho_1}{\sqrt{1 - .64\rho_1^2}}$$

For example, if the correlation between test and job performance in the applicant population were .50, then the correlation in the study population would be

$$\rho_2 = \frac{.60(.50)}{\sqrt{1 - .64(.50)^2}} = \frac{.60(.50)}{.92} = .33$$

That is, if the study is done on only the top half of the distribution on the independent variable, then the population correlation would be reduced from .50 to .33. If undetected, this difference between .50 and .33 would have profound implications for the interpretation of empirical studies.

But suppose we have the data, i.e., $\rho_2 = .33$ and $u = .60$, and we wish to correct for restriction in range. We could reverse the roles of the two populations. That is, we could regard the applicant population as an enhancement of the incumbent population. We could then use the same formula above with roles, reversed, i.e.,

$$\rho_1 = \frac{U\rho_2}{\sqrt{(U^2 - 1)\rho_2^2 + 1}}$$

where

$$U = \frac{\sigma_{x_1}}{\sigma_{x_2}} = \frac{1}{u}$$

is the ratio of standard deviations in the opposite order. This formula is called the correction for restriction in range, though it would also work for correction for enhancement. In the personnel example, we plug in $\rho_1 = .33$ and $U = 1/u = 1/.60 = 1.67$ to obtain

$$\rho_1 = \frac{1.67(.33)}{\sqrt{(1.67^2 - 1)(.33)^2 + 1}} = \frac{1.67(.33)}{1.09} = .50$$

Thus at the level of population correlations, we can use the formula for restriction in range to move back and forth between populations of different variance without error.

The situation is more complicated if there is sampling error. If we apply the formula for correction for restriction in range to a sample correlation, then we get only an approximation to the reference group population correlation. Moreover, the corrected correlation will have a different amount of sampling error. This situation is analogous to that in correction for attenuation. There is a tradeoff; in order to eliminate the systematic error associated with restriction in range, we must accept the increase in sampling error that goes with the statistical correction formula. If we could correct substantively, i.e., if the study could be made on the reference population, then there would be no increase in sampling error. In fact, in the case of restriction in range, the study done on the applicant population (if it could be done) would have the larger correlation and hence the smaller confidence interval.

The confidence interval for the corrected correlation is easy to obtain. The correction formula can be regarded as a mathematical transformation. This transformation is monotone and hence it transforms confidence intervals. Thus the confidence interval is obtained by correcting the endpoints of the confidence interval using the same formula that is used to correct the correlation. That is, the same range correction formula is applied to the endpoints of the confidence interval as is applied to the correlation itself.

Consider the personnel example in which the population correlations are .50 for the applicant population and .33 for the study population. If the sample size is 100, then the sampling error for a correlation of $\rho = .33$ is $\sigma_e = (1 - .33^2)/\sqrt{99} = .09$. If the sample correlation came out low, it might be something such as .28, which is low by .05. Corrected for restriction in range of $U = 1.67$ we have

$$r_c = \frac{1.67(.28)}{\sqrt{(1.67^2 - 1)(.28^2) + 1}} = \frac{.47}{1.07} = .44$$

Lower Endpoint	Upper Endpoint
$r_1 = .10$	$r_2 = .46$

$$r_{c_1} = \frac{1.67(.10)}{\sqrt{(1.67^2 - 1).10^2 + 1}} \qquad r_{c_2} = \frac{1.67(.46)}{\sqrt{(1.67^2 - 1).46^2 + 1}}$$

$$= .16 \qquad\qquad\qquad = .65$$

Thus the confidence interval for the corrected correlation is $.16 \leqslant \rho_c \leqslant .65$, which includes the actual value of $\rho_c = .50$. This confidence interval is much wider than the confidence interval for the uncorrected correlation and wider yet than the confidence interval that would have been found had the study been done in the reference population itself.

RANGE CORRECTION AND SAMPLING ERROR

There is no difficulty in obtaining a confidence interval for a corrected correlation using the range correction formula; we simply correct the two endpoints of the confidence interval for the uncorrected correlation. However, it is not so easy to compute the standard deviation of the sampling error. Correction for attenuation is a linear operation; the uncorrected correlation is just multiplied by a constant. Thus the sampling error and the error standard deviation are multiplied by the same constant. However, the range correction formula is not linear and there is no known formula for the resulting standard deviation. The extent of nonlinearity depends on the size of the numbers involved, i.e., the extent to which U is different from 1 and the extent to which the uncorrected correlation has a square much greater than 0. If the nonlinearity is not too great, then we can approximate the sampling error by pretending that we have just multiplied the uncorrected correlation by the constant

$$\alpha = \frac{r_c}{r}$$

The sampling error would then be approximately

$$\sigma_{e_c}^2 = \alpha^2 \sigma_e^2$$

To see the extent of this approximation, let us consider our personnel research example. We center our confidence interval for the corrected correlation about the corrected correlation itself, i.e., around $r_o = .44$. The error standard deviation for the uncorrected correlation is $(1 - .28^2)/\sqrt{99} = .093$ and the ratio of corrected to uncorrected correlations is $.44/.28 = 1.57$. Hence the estimated error standard deviation for the corrected correlation is $(1.57)(.093) = .146$. The corresponding confidence interval is $.15 \leqslant \rho_c \leqslant .73$. This implied confidence interval differs only slightly from the confidence interval obtained by correcting the endpoints; i.e., $.16 \leqslant \rho_c \leqslant .65$.

An Example: Confidence Intervals

Consider a personnel selection validation study. Given an observed correlation of .30 with a sample size of 100, the confidence interval for the uncorrected validity coefficient is $P[.12 \leqslant \rho \leqslant .48] = .95$. From King, Hunter, and Schmidt (1980), we know that the reliability of the supervisor ratings is at most .60. If the selection ratio is 50 percent, then the formulas in Schmidt, Hunter, and Urry (1976) show that the ratio of the standard deviation of the application group to that of the incumbent population is 1.67. The point correction of the observed validity coefficient is therefore:

$$r_1 = \frac{1.67r}{\sqrt{(1.67^2 - 1)r^2 + 1}} = .46$$

$$r_2 = \frac{r_1}{\sqrt{.60}} = .60$$

The confidence interval for the corrected validity is obtained by applying the same corrections to the endpoints of the confidence interval for the uncorrected validity.

Lower Endpoint   Upper Endpoint

$$r_1 = \frac{1.67(.12)}{\sqrt{(1.67^2 - 1).12^2 + 1}} \qquad r_1 = \frac{1.67(.48)}{\sqrt{(1.67^2 - 1).48^2 + 1}}$$

$$= .20 \qquad\qquad\qquad = .67$$

$$r_2 = \frac{.20}{\sqrt{.60}} = .26 \qquad\qquad r_2 = \frac{.67}{\sqrt{.60}} = .86$$

Hence the confidence interval for the corrected validity is

$$P\left\{ .26 \leqslant \rho \leqslant .86 \right\} = .95$$

RANGE RESTRICTION AND THE SELECTION RATIO

In personnel research, the restriction in range often comes about in a very particular way: People are hired from the top down using the test that is to be validated. Only those hired appear in the validation study. Thus those who appear in the study are chosen from the top portion of the reference population distribution of test scores. Since test score distributions in applicant populations are normal distributions, this means that the range restriction parameter u can be computed indirectly from the selection ratio.

The selection ratio is defined as the proportion of applicants selected by the test. For example, if applicants are hired only if they are in the top tenth of the distribution, then the selection ratio is 10 percent. The test selection ratio will be equal to the percentage of applicants hired if hiring is done solely on test scores. If additional requirements are imposed, then it is the test ratio that should be used. For example, police departments require applicants to pass a medical exam, a psychiatric exam, and a background investigation in addition to the selection test. Typically, about two-thirds of the applicants checked fail one or the other of these additional checks. Thus if the proportion of persons hired is 13 percent, then the test selection ratio is 39 percent.

Let p be the selection ratio as a proportion (i.e., as a fraction such as .10, rather than a percentage). If we are hiring from the top of a normal distribution, then corresponding to any selection ratio p there is a cutoff score C such that

$$P\,[x \geqslant C] = p$$

If that cutoff score is given in standard score form, then it can be looked up using the normal distribution table backwards. Once the cutoff score is known, then we can compute the mean and variance in test scores among those selected in standard score form using the following formulas

$$\mu_x = \frac{\phi(C)}{p}$$

where $\phi(C)$ is the value of the normal density function at the cutoff (also called the "normal ordinate" above (C) and

$$\sigma_x^2 = 1 - \mu_x(\mu_x - C) = 1 - \mu_x^2 + C\mu_x$$

Since the applicant population has a variance of 1 in standard scores, the number σ_x is equal to the parameter u in the range restriction formula.

For example, if the selection ratio is 10 percent, then the normal distribution table shows that a cutoff score of 1.28 is required to select the top tenth. The mean standard score among those selected will be

$$\mu_x = \frac{1}{p} \; \frac{1}{\sqrt{2\pi}} \; e^{-C^2/2} = 10 \; \frac{1}{2.507} \; e^{-.82} = 1.76$$

The variance among those selected is

$$\sigma_x^2 = 1 - 1.76^2 + 1.28(1.76) = .1552$$

The standard deviation and hence the parameter u is then the square root of .1552, which is .39. That is, with a selection ratio of 10 percent, the standard deviation in the study population will be less than half the standard deviation in the applicant population.

META-ANALYSIS OF CORRECTED CORRELATIONS

In this section we assume that each study contains all the information required to correct each correlation for attenuation due to error of measurement in both variables and to correct the correlation for restriction in range in the independent variable if necessary. Basically, the mathematics is derived by multiplying each sampling error standard deviation by the ratio of the corrected to uncorrected correlation. However, we should note at the outset that this method can only occasionally be used. Most studies do not provide reliability information, and most studies do not provide the standard deviations needed to correct for restriction in range. We will later provide distributional formulas that may be used when artifact data is only sporadically given.

Most correlations are suppressed from their true values by error of measurement in one or both variables. If the amount of error is known in the form of the reliabilities of each variable, then an estimate of the correlation between true scores is given by the formula for correction for attenuation:

$$r_c = \alpha_1 r$$

where r is the observed correlation, r_c is the corrected correlation, and

$$\alpha_1 = \frac{1}{\sqrt{r_{xx} r_{yy}}}$$

where r_{xx} and r_{yy} are the reliabilities of x and y, respectively. If error in only one of the variables is to be corrected, then the other reliability is omitted from α_1. The sampling error in the corrected correlation is related to the sampling error in the uncorrected correlation by the linearity of the correction based on

$$\sigma_c^2 = \alpha_1^2 \sigma_c^2 = \alpha_1^2 \frac{(1 - \rho^2)^2}{N - 1}$$

It is often the case that observations must be made on populations different from that to which inference is desired. For example, in industrial psychology, job performance can be measured only on those who are hired, i.e., incumbents, while for utility analyses and other purposes the desired correlation is that for the entire applicant pool. If the range variation is caused by variation on only one of the variables being correlated (i.e., the selection test in the industrial example), and if the standard deviations for that variable on both populations is known, then the observed correlation can be corrected for the attenuation effect of restriction in range produced by the selection:

$$r_c = \alpha_2 r$$

where

$$\alpha_2 = \frac{u}{\sqrt{(u^2 - 1) r^2 + 1}}$$

where

$$u = \frac{\sigma \text{ in the reference population}}{\sigma \text{ in the study population}}$$

The presence of the term "r^2" in the denominator of α_2 means that the correction formula is not strictly linear. However, if r is small (i.e., in which case r^2 is very small) or if the standard deviation ratio u does not differ too severely from 1, then the departure from linearity is negligible. Thus to a good approximation, the sampling error is given by the formula

$$\sigma_{e_c}^2 = \alpha_2^2 \sigma_e^2$$

Both the correction for restriction in range and the correction for attenuation due to measurement error are often necessary. The two corrections can be made one after the other in a certain order. If the reliability is calculated on the study group, then the correction for attenuation should be done before correction for restriction in range. If the reliability is known for the reference population, then correction for restriction in range should be made first. In either case, we have

$$r_c = \alpha r$$

where the unsubscripted α is the ratio of corrected to uncorrected correlations, and the approximation

$$\sigma_{e_c}^2 = \alpha^2 \sigma_e^2$$

estimates the sampling error of the corrected correlation. If we represent the sampling in the corrected correlation by e_{c_i} and the corrected population correlation by ρ_i, then

$$r_{c_i} = \rho_i + e_{c_i}$$

and

$$\sigma_c^2 = \sigma_\rho^2 + \sigma_{e_c}^2$$

where

$$\sigma_{e_c}^2 = \alpha^2 \frac{(1 - r^2)^2}{N_i - 1}$$

The total error variance for frequency weighted distribution of the corrected correlations is then given by

$$\sigma_{e_c}^2 = \frac{1}{N} \sum_i N_i \alpha_i^2 \frac{(1 - r_i^2)^2}{N_i - 1}$$

If the correction factors α_i vary only slightly from the mean $\bar{\alpha}$, then a good approximation for this sampling error is given by

$$\sigma_{e_c}^2 = \bar{\alpha}^2 \frac{K(1 - \bar{r}^2)^2}{N}$$

which is simply $\bar{\alpha}^2$ times the estimated error variance for uncorrected correlations. This then yields the following estimate of the variance of population correlations, if any:

$$\sigma_{\rho_c}^2 = \sigma_{r_c}^2 - \sigma_{e_c}^2$$

An Example: Validity Generalization

Validation studies are usually done on incumbent worker populations that have been selected using either the same or a similar test to that being validated. Thus they are subject to sometimes extreme restriction of range. Criterion measures may have high reliability (job knowledge tests or training school scores) or low reliability (supervisor ratings). Thus observed validity coefficients are subject to both restriction in range and to error of measurement. Table 3.4 presents a hypothetical set of validity coefficients generated by assuming that all population correlations are the same, $\rho = .50$; then reducing the correlation according to the degree of unreliability and restriction of range shown and then adding sampling error. The observed correlations are then corrected using the usual formulas. The criterion reliabilities are values for the applicant pool; therefore, range restriction corrections are made first, then reliability corrections. For comparison purposes, sampling error corrections are made for the observed correlations as well as for the corrected correlations.

Uncorrected Correlations	Corrected Correlations
$\bar{r} = .28$	$\bar{r} = .49$
$\sigma_r^2 = .01703$	$\sigma_r^2 = .03985$
$\sigma_e^2 = .01249$	$\sigma_e^2 = .04637$
$\sigma_\rho^2 = .00454$	$\sigma_\rho^2 = -.0065$
$SD_\rho = .07$	$SD_\rho = 0$

Calculations.

Uncorrected Correlations

$$\sigma_e^2 = \frac{(1 - .28^2)^2(12)}{816}$$

$$\sigma_e^2 = .01249$$

$$\sigma_\rho^2 = .01703 - .01249$$

$$\sigma_\rho^2 = .0045$$

Corrected Correlations

$$\sigma_e^2 = \frac{3.71(1 - .28^2)^2(12)}{816}$$

$$\sigma_e^2 = .04633$$

$$\sigma_\rho^2 = .03985 - .04633$$

$$\sigma_\rho^2 = -.0065$$

TABLE 3.4 Hypothetical Validity Coefficients

Selection Ratio	u	Criterion Reliability	Sample Size	Observed Correlation	Corrected Correlation	α^2
.20	.468	.80	68	.35**	.70	4.00
.20	.468	.60	68	.07	.19	7.37
.20	.468	.80	68	.11	.26	5.59
.20	.468	.60	68	.31*	.74	5.70
.50	.603	.80	68	.18	.32	3.16
.50	.603	.60	68	.36**	.71	3.89
.50	.603	.80	68	.40**	.66	2.72
.50	.603	.60	68	.13	.27	4.31
.90	.844	.80	68	.49**	.62	1.60
.90	.844	.60	68	.23	.35	2.32
.90	.844	.80	68	.29*	.38	1.72
.90	.844	.60	68	.44**	.65	2.18

*p < .05 (2-tailed).
**p < .01 (2-tailed).
$\bar{\alpha}^2$ = 3.71.

The results for uncorrected correlations show an incorrect mean of .28 (versus the true value of .50), and the remaining variation across studies is all artifactual, that is, the uncorrected correlations vary due to differential range restriction and criterion unreliability. The results for corrected correlations show an almost correct mean of .49 and correctly indicate that there is no variation across studies.

ARTIFACT DISTRIBUTIONS

The preceding section assumed that the correlation in each individual study could be corrected for artifacts. However, it is a rare study that provides all the information required to correct for attenuation in both variables and to correct for restriction in range where applicable. Instead, one study will give one reliability, another study will give another and occasional studies will present standard deviations that permit assessment of departure in range. It is not uncommon to find that no single study provides all the necessary information.

On the other hand, the set of studies may provide distributional information about all the artifacts. That is, just as we compile information about the distribution of the correlation r_{xy}, so too we can compile information about the distribution of the reliability of the independent variable r_{xx}, the distribution of the reliability of the dependent variable r_{yy}, and the extent of restriction range u (defined as the ratio of the standard deviation of x in the group studied to the standard deviation in the reference population). If the artifacts are independently distributed, these distributional facts can be used to estimate the distribution of the corrected population correlations that is desired.

Basically, the strategy is this. In the previous section we first corrected each correlation and then computed the mean and variance of corrected correlations. In this section, we will reverse that order. We will first compute the average and the variance of the uncorrected correlations. We will then correct the average and the variance to eliminate the effects of the various artifacts.

Formulas for this were first developed in the specialized area of personnel selection research under the rubric "validity generalization" (Schmidt and Hunter, 1977). However, there are certain quirks to research in personnel selection. Although restriction in range is always present, there are reasons for not correcting for error of measurement in x. As a result, the formulas from validity generalization must be modified to be useful in a more general context. We will develop three sets of formulas here. First, we will consider the most common case: error of measurement in both variables x and y, but no restriction in range. We will then develop a set of formulas for the case in which all three artifacts are to be eliminated. Finally, we will present the validity generalization formulas as they are currently used in personnel selection research. Thus we exactly reverse the historical order in which the formulas were developed.

ARTIFACT DISTRIBUTIONS: ERROR OF MEASUREMENT

Variables in the social sciences are often only poorly measured. Thus we would only expect uniformity in the literature if results are corrected to eliminate error of measurement. In this case we must not only distinguish between population and sample statistics, but also between observed scores and true scores. Let the perfectly measured version of the observed independent variable x be denoted T and let the perfectly measured version of the observed dependent variable y be denoted U. For each study, there are two unknown population correlations ρ_{xy} and ρ_{TU} and one known sample correlation r_{xy}. Error of measurement is measured by the two reliabilities that apply to that study: r_{xx} and r_{yy}. One might think that the reliabilities would be constant across studies, but most areas have not standardized measurement procedures. Even with a variable such as authoritarianism, the F scale may be the base measurement procedure, but each individual study may use a different subset of the items from that scale. Ideally each study would report the reliability of each scale used (using an estimate such as Cronbach's [1951] coefficient alpha), but in practice this is just not so. Thus we must search for studies that report reliabilities just as we search for studies that report correlations.

The unknown population correlations are related by the attenuation equation

$$\rho_{xy} = \sqrt{r_{xx}} \sqrt{r_{yy}} \, \rho_{TU}$$

The observed sample correlation is related to the unknown population correlations by

$$r_{xy} = \rho_{xy} + e = \sqrt{r_{xx}} \sqrt{r_{yy}} \, \rho_{TU} + e$$

where e is the sampling error in the observed correlation. If we focus on the population correlation between observed scores ρ_{xy}, then our analysis is just as before since we are eliminating only the effect of sampling error.

$$\bar{r}_{xy} = \bar{\rho}_{xy}$$

$$\sigma^2_{r_{xy}} = \sigma^2_{\rho_{xy}} + \sigma^2_e$$

where as before

$$\sigma_e^2 = \frac{K(1 - \bar{r}^2)^2}{N}$$

where K is the number of studies and N is the total sample size across studies. The corrected variance formula now yields

$$\sigma_r^2 - \sigma_e^2 = \sigma_\rho^2 = \sigma_{\rho_{xy}}^2$$

The question is: How do we go from these statistics on the distribution of ρ_{xy} to the statistics on the distribution of the desired correlation ρ_{TU}? The key is to use the knowledge about the distribution of reliabilities to correct the mean and variance of ρ_{xy} for the effects of attenuation. To do so we will make three assumptions: (1) the distribution of reliabilities of the independent variable in studies in which it is not reported is the same as it is in those in which it is reported, (2) the distribution of reliabilities of the dependent variable in studies in which it is not reported is the same as it is in those in which it is reported, and (3) the reliabilities in a given study are independent of the correlation between true scores.

To simply the algebra below, let us introduce a notation similar to that of Callender and Osburn (1980); let us denote the square root of r_{xx} by a, the square root of r_{yy} by b, and use the symbol ρ for ρ_{TU}. We can then relate the population correlation for observed scores to the desired population correlation between true scores ρ_{TU} (or just ρ in the reduced notation) as a triple product

$$\rho_{xy} = ab\rho$$

The standard meta-analysis procedures produce the numbers ρ_{xy} and $\sigma_{\rho_{xy}}^2$, which will then be related to the desired $\bar{\rho}$ and σ_ρ^2 by formulas for the mean and variance of a triple product. The key to this development is the assumption that a, b, and ρ are independent.

Consider the product of three variables a, b, and c. If these variables are independent, then the mean of the product is the product of the means, i.e.,

$$E[abc] = E[a] \ E[b] \ E[c]$$

If three variables are independent, then so are their squares. Hence

$$E[a^2b^2c^2] = E[a^2] \ E[b^2] \ E[c^2]$$

For any variable, there is a relationship between its variance, it mean, and its mean square. The conventional form of this relationship is used to compute the variance

$$\sigma_x^2 = E[x^2] - (E[x])^2 = E[x^2] - \bar{x}^2$$

but which is also useful in the reordered form

$$E[x^2] = \bar{x}^2 + \sigma_x^2$$

We can now derive a formula for the variance of a triple product if all three variables are independent.

$$
\begin{aligned}
\sigma_{abc}^2 &= E[(abc)^2] - (E[abc])^2 \\
&= E[a^2b^2c^2] - (E[a] \ E[b] \ E[c])^2 \\
&= E[a^2] \ E[b^2] \ E[c^2] - \bar{a}^2 \ \bar{b}^2 \ \bar{c}^2 \\
&= (\bar{a}^2 + \sigma_a^2)(\bar{b}^2 + \sigma_b^2)(\bar{c}^2 + \sigma_c^2) - \bar{a}^2 \ \bar{b}^2 \ \bar{c}^2 \\
&= \bar{a}^2 \ \bar{b}^2 \ \sigma_c^2 + \bar{a}^2 \ \bar{c}^2 \ \sigma_b^2 + \bar{b}^2 \ \bar{c}^2 \ \sigma_a^2 \\
&\quad + \bar{a}^2 \ \sigma_b^2 \ \sigma_c^2 + \bar{b}^2 \ \sigma_a^2 \ \sigma_c^2 + \bar{c}^2 \ \sigma_a^2 \ \sigma_b^2 \\
&\quad + \sigma_a^2 \ \sigma_b^2 \ \sigma_c^2
\end{aligned}
$$

The terms in this variance have been listed in a special order: The first three terms have two means and one variance, the next three terms have one mean and two variances, and the last term is the product of three variances. The order is important because in our context, the variables, a, b, and c are all fractions and have means much larger than variances. Thus the last four terms in our formula are negligible in size.

To see this, consider the variable a, which is the square root of the reliability of the independent variable. A typical reliability distribution might have a mean of .60 and an effective range of .40 to .80, i.e., a mean of .60 and a standard deviation of .10. The square root of the reliability would have a mean of about .77 and an effective range of .63 to .89, i.e., a mean of .77 and a standard deviation of .065. If we compare square of means and variances, then we see that for a typical distribution of variable a, we have $\bar{a}^2 = .60$ and $\sigma_a^2 = .0042$. By using the ratio to compare these numbers, we see that the variance is less than $1/100$ of the square of the mean.

In the triple product, we have $\rho_{xy} = abc$ where $c = \rho_{TU}$. Thus for all practical purposes, the assumption of independence in our situation means that

$$\bar{\rho}_{xy} = \bar{a}\,\bar{b}\,\bar{\rho}_{TU}$$

$$\sigma^2_{\rho_{xy}} = \bar{a}^2\,\bar{b}^2\,\bar{\sigma}_\rho^2 + \bar{\rho}_{TU}^2\,\bar{a}^2\,\bar{\sigma}_b^2 + \bar{\rho}_{TU}^2\,\bar{b}^2\,\bar{\sigma}_a^2$$

If we reverse the first equation, then we see that the desired mean true score correlation is given by

$$\bar{\rho}_{TU} = \frac{\bar{\rho}_{xy}}{\bar{a}\bar{b}}$$

To a close approximation, this equation amounts to correcting average uncorrected correlation for attenuation using the average reliabilites. If we reverse the second equation, we have the desired variance of the true score correlations

$$\sigma^2_{\rho_{TU}} = \frac{\sigma^2_{\rho_{xy}} - \bar{\rho}^2_{TU}(\bar{a}^2 \, \sigma^2_b + \bar{b}^2 \, \sigma^2_a)}{\bar{a}^2 \, \bar{b}^2}$$

To summarize . . . If either the independent variable or the dependent variable is imperfectly measured, then the correlation between the imperfectly measured variables will be systematically lower than the correlation between true scores. If we knew the reliability for both variables in each study, then we could eliminate the effect of error of measurement in each study by correcting for attenuation:

$$\hat{r}_{TU} = \frac{r_{xy}}{\sqrt{r_{xx}} \, \sqrt{r_{yy}}}$$

The average of these corrected correlations across studies would estimate the desired average correlation $\bar{\rho}_{TU}$. The variance of the corrected correlations could be corrected for sampling error as in the immediately preceding section to provide the desired variance of population correlations $\sigma^2_{\rho_{TU}}$.

However, if we cannot correct correlations for error of measurement separately, then we can use special meta-analysis formulas to obtain the same numbers from knowledge of the distribution of r_{xy}, the distribution of r_{xx}, and the distribution of r_{yy}. First, we compile studies that have estimates of *any* of the three numbers r_{xy}, r_{xx}, or r_{yy}. We take square roots of r_{xx} and r_{yy}, which we call a and b, respectively. We then go across the studies three times to compile distributions for r_{xy}, a, and b separately. That is, using data from whichever studies have it, we compute three means and three variances: $\bar{r}_{xy}$ and $\sigma^2_{r_{xy}}$ from studies with r_{xy}, $\bar{a}$ and σ^2_a from those studies with r_{xx}, and b and σ^2_b from those studies with r_{yy}.

The next step is to eliminate the effects of sampling error. This is the usual first step in meta-analysis. First, to the extent that the total sample size is large, there is little sampling error in the average correlation. Thus we estimate $\bar{\rho}_{xy} = \bar{r}_{xy}$. However, the variance is considerably inflated by sampling error. So we compute the sampling error variance σ_e^2 and subtract. That is, our estimates of the distribution of population correlations between observed scores are

$$\bar{\rho}_{xy} = \bar{r}_{xy}$$

$$\sigma_{\rho_{xy}}^2 = \sigma_{r_{xy}}^2 - \sigma_e^2$$

The next step is to eliminate the effects of error of measurement. This involves two steps: elimination of the systematic downward bias in the average correlation and elimination of the variance across studies due to the variation in reliability from one study to the next. To do this we use the reliability distributions for a and b computed in the first step.

$$\bar{\rho}_{TU} = \frac{\bar{\rho}_{xy}}{\bar{a}\bar{b}}$$

$$\sigma_{\rho_{TU}}^2 = \frac{\sigma_{\rho_{xy}}^2 - \bar{\rho}_{TU}^2 (\bar{a}^2 \sigma_b^2 + \bar{b}^2 \sigma_a^2)}{\bar{a}^2 \bar{b}^2}$$

These two numbers now describe the distribution of population correlations between the independent and dependent variables had the studies been done with perfect measurement. If there is no reason to suspect serious amounts of range variation across studies, then this would be the endpoint of the meta-analysis procedure.

If the studies are broken down to check for a moderator variable, then a new mean and variance would be computed for the correlations across each subset of the data. However, the overall distributions would still be used for the reliability distributions. That is, the same overall means and variances for a

TABLE 3.5   Organizational Commitment and Job Satisfaction

	Organizational Commitment Reliability (r_{xx})	Job Satisfaction Reliability (r_{yy})	Sample Size (N_i)	Sample Correlation (r_{xy})
Ermine (1976)	.70			
Ferret (1977)	.50			
Mink (1976)		.70		
Otter (1977)		.50		
Polecat (1978)			68	.01
Stoat (1979)			68	.14
Weasel (1980)			68	.23*
Wolverine (1978)			68	.34**

*Significant at the .05 level.
**Significant at the .01 level.

and b would be used to do the meta-analysis in each subset of studies.

If the set of studies is subject to range variation, then correction for error of measurement must be done in conjunction with correction for range variation. This will be taken up in the next several sections of this chapter.

Artifactual Distributions Example:
Organizational Commitment and Job Satisfaction

Table 3.5 presents findings from a hypothetical set of studies related to organizational commitment and job satisfaction. The studies are listed in three groups. The first pair of studies presents no correlational data pertaining to organizational commitment or job satisfaction, but these studies do contain reliability data on organizational commitment. The first is the classic study in which Ermine presented his measure of organization commitment. The second study is one in which Ferret used "the key items from Ermine" and then correlated commitment with other variables (not including job satisfaction). The second pair of studies contains only reliability information on job satisfaction.

Finally, the last four studies contain only correlational information (although each study had the item data and hence could have computed reliability coefficients for that study).

In Table 3.5 we see that two of the correlations were significant while two were not. If we properly eliminate the effects of sampling error, we have

$$\bar{\rho}_{xy} = \bar{r} = .18$$

$$\sigma_r^2 = .01465$$

$$\sigma_e^2 = \frac{4(1 - .18^2)^2}{272} = .01377$$

$$\sigma_{\rho_{xy}}^2 = \sigma_r^2 - \sigma_e^2 = .01465 - .01377 = .00088$$

$$\sigma_{\rho_{xy}} = .03$$

This analysis of sampling error shows that there is little variation in the correlations across studies. The 95 percent probability interval is $.12 \leqslant \rho_{xy} \leqslant .24$. Thus the two studies that fail to find statistical significance contain Type II errors.

To eliminate the artifacts due to error of measurement, we first find the means and standard deviations of the product variables a and b and the square roots of the reliabilities.

$$\bar{a} = \frac{\sqrt{.70} + \sqrt{.50}}{2} = \frac{.84 + .71}{2} = .775$$

$$\sigma_a^2 = \frac{(.84 - .775)^2 + (.71 - .775)^2}{2} = .0042$$

$$\bar{b} = .775$$

$$\sigma_b^2 = .0042$$

Now we can find the distribution of true score correlations:

$$\bar{\rho}_{TU} = \frac{\bar{P}_{xy}}{\bar{a}\bar{b}} = \frac{.18}{(.775)(.775)} = \frac{.18}{.60} = .30$$

$$\sigma^2_{\rho_{TU}} = \frac{\sigma^2_{P_{xy}} - \bar{\rho}^2_{TU}(\bar{a}^2\,\sigma^2_b + \bar{b}^2\,\sigma^2_a)}{\bar{a}^2\,\bar{b}^2}$$

$$= \frac{.00088 - (.30)^2\{(.775)^2(.0042) + (.775)^2(.0042)\}}{(.775)^2(.775)^2}$$

$$= \frac{.00088 - .00045}{.36} = .00119$$

$$\sigma_{\rho_{TU}} = .03$$

$$.24 \leqslant \rho \leqslant .36$$

Let us consider the impact of artifacts in this example. The impact of sampling error on the mean correlation was assumed to be negligible (though that would not really be true with a total sample size of only 272). However, the impact of sampling error on the variance across studies is massive: The variance of the sample correlations is .01465, of which sampling error is .01377, variance due to variation of reliability is .00045, and "else" is .00043. That is, 94 percent of the variance in correlations across studies is due to sampling error, 3 percent is due to variation in reliability, and 3 percent is due to unspecified other determinants.

On the other hand, the impact of error of measurement is largely on the mean correlation. The error of measurement caused the mean correlation to be depressed from .30 to .18.

ARTIFACT DISTRIBUTIONS:
UNRELIABILITY AND RANGE VARIATION

If studies are subject to range variation, then there are four population correlations of interest: the correlation between observed scores in the reference and study populations and the correlation between true scores in the reference and study populations. In order to eliminate needless profusion of notation, we will refer to only two of these correlations in this section. We will use ρ_{xy} for the population correlation between observed scores in the study population, and we will use ρ_{TU} for the desired correlation between true scores in the reference population. The observed study correlation is related to the population correlation by the equation

$$r_{xy} = \rho_{xy} + e$$

where e is the sampling error in the observed correlation, and

$$\rho_{xy} = abc\,\rho_{TU}$$

where

$$a = \sqrt{r_{xx}}$$

$$b = \sqrt{r_{yy}}$$

$$c = \frac{u}{\sqrt{(u^2 - 1)\rho_1^2 + 1}}$$

where

$$u = \frac{\sigma_T \text{ on the study population}}{\sigma_T \text{ on the reference population}}$$

$$\rho_1^2 = r_{xx} r_{yy} \rho_{TU}^2$$

These equations suggest a two-step procedure for correcting for artifacts: First, use the first equation to correct the variance for sampling error as we have done before. Second, use the product equation to correct the mean correlation and to correct the variance for the other three artifacts. However, there is a rub in the second step; the factor c contains ρ_{TU}^2 in the denominator. Thus factors c and ρ_{TU} are not independent. However, the degree of dependence is slight and simulation studies have shown the error in assuming independence to be trivial in magnitude (e.g., Callender & Osburn, 1980). The formulas below make the independence assumption for all four factors.

Consider the product of four independent variables abcd. Using the methods of the previous section we obtain the following key formulas.

$$E\,[abcd] = E\,[a]\;E\,[b]\;E\,[c]\;E\,[d] = \bar{a}\bar{b}\bar{c}\bar{d}$$

$$\sigma_{abcd}^2 = \bar{a}^2\bar{b}^2\bar{c}^2\,\sigma_d^2 + \bar{b}^2\bar{c}^2\bar{d}^2\,\sigma_a^2 + \bar{a}^2\bar{b}^2\bar{d}^2\,\sigma_c^2 + \bar{a}^2\bar{c}^2\bar{d}^2\,\sigma_b^2$$

+ terms with two or more variances

The corresponding correction formulas are

$$\bar{\rho}_{TU} = \frac{\bar{r}_{xy}}{\bar{a}\bar{b}\bar{c}}$$

$$\sigma_{\rho_{TU}}^2 = \frac{\sigma_{\rho_{xy}}^2 - \bar{\rho}_{TU}^2(\bar{b}^2\bar{c}^2\,\sigma_a^2 + \bar{a}^2\bar{c}^2\,\sigma_b^2 + \bar{a}^2\bar{b}^2\,\sigma_c^2)}{\bar{a}^2\bar{b}^2\bar{c}^2}$$

The correction formula for the mean differs little from correcting the mean observed correlation using the mean reliability of the independent variable, the mean reliability of the dependent variable, and the mean extent of range change.

In computing the mean and variance for factors a and b, it is important to remember to use the square roots of the reliabilities rather than the reliabilities themselves. To compute the factor c, we must first compute the ratio u, the ratio of the standard deviation of the study population to the standard deviation of the reference population. The defining formula for c above requires knowledge of ρ_1^2, which is not given in the data for single studies. Instead, we use an identity from Callender and Osburn (1980):

$$c = \sqrt{u^2 + (1 - u^2)\rho_{xy}^2}$$

This formula involves ρ_{xy}, which is not given in the data for single studies either. Instead, we use the approximation $\rho_{xy}^2 = \bar{r}_{xy}^2$. That is, we estimate c by substituting the observed mean $\bar{r}$ for ρ_{xy}.

To summarize . . . If we do not have the data to correct correlations individually, then we must use the meta-analysis formulas based on distributions of artifacts. If we are to correct sampling error, error of measurement in both variables, and for range variation, then we first compile information across studies on four statistics: the distribution of the observed correlation r_{xy}, the reliability of the independent variable r_{xx}, the reliability of the dependent variable r_{yy}, and the extent of range departure u. From these we compute four means and variances: the mean and variance of the four statistics r_{xy}, a, b, and c. We then take two steps to use these statistics to compute the mean and variance of the population correlation between true scores on the reference population. The first step is to correct the mean and variance of observed correlations for sampling error:

$$\bar{\rho}_{xy} = \bar{r}_{xy}$$

$$\sigma_{\rho_{xy}}^2 = \sigma_{r_{xy}}^2 - \sigma_e^2$$

TABLE 3.6   Sixteen Hypothetical Studies

	N	r_{xx}	r_{yy}	u	r_{xy}	a	b	c
(1)	68	.49	—	.40	.02	.70	—	.43
(2)	68	—	.64	—	.26*	—	.80	—
(3)	68	.49	.64	—	.33*	.70	.80	—
(4)	68	—	—	.60	.09	—	—	.62
(5)	68	.49	—	—	.02	.70	—	—
(6)	68	—	.49	.40	.24*	—	.70	.43
(7)	68	.49	.49	—	.30*	.70	.70	—
(8)	68	—	—	.60	.06	—	—	.62
(9)	68	.64	—	.40	.28*	.80	—	.43
(10)	68	—	.64	—	.04	—	.80	—
(11)	68	.64	.64	—	.12	.80	.80	—
(12)	68	—	—	.60	.34*	—	—	.62
(13)	68	.64	—	—	.26*	.80	—	—
(14)	68	—	.49	.40	.02	—	.70	.43
(15)	68	.64	.49	—	.09	.80	.70	—
(16)	68	—	—	.60	.33*	—	—	.62

*Significant at the .05 level, 2-tailed test.

The second step is to correct the sampling error corrected mean and variance for the effect of the other three artifacts:

$$\bar{\rho}_{TU} = \frac{\bar{\rho}_{xy}}{\bar{a}\,\bar{b}\,\bar{c}}$$

$$\sigma^2_{\rho_{TU}} = \frac{\sigma^2_{\rho_{xy}} - \bar{\rho}^2_{TU}(\bar{b}^2\bar{c}^2\sigma^2_a + \bar{a}^2\bar{c}^2\sigma^2_b + \bar{a}^2\bar{b}^2\sigma^2_c)}{\bar{a}^2\bar{b}^2\bar{c}^2}$$

An Example: Correcting for Sampling Error, Error of Measurement, and Range Variation with Sporadic Artifact Information

The example in Table 3.6 was created by assuming that the population correlation between true scores in the reference population is always $\rho_{TU} = .60$. The first five columns of Table 3.6

are the data extracted from the sixteen hypothetical studies. The last three columns are the values of a, b, and c computed from the values of r_{xx}, r_{yy}, and u, respectively.

The four means and variances needed are:

$$\bar{r} = .175 \qquad \bar{a} = .75 \qquad \bar{b} = .75 \qquad \bar{c} = .525$$

$$\sigma_r^2 = .015100 \qquad \sigma_a^2 = .0025 \qquad \sigma_b^2 = .0025 \qquad \sigma_c^2 = .0090$$

We first use the mean and variance of the observed correlations to correct for sampling error:

$$\bar{\rho}_{xy} = \bar{r} = .175$$

$$\sigma_{\rho_{xy}}^2 = \sigma_r^2 - \sigma_e^2 = .015100 - 013819 = .001281$$

These values can then be corrected to eliminate the effects of error of measurement and range variation:

$$\bar{\rho}_{TU} = \frac{.175}{(.75)(.75)(.525)} = .59$$

$$\sigma_{\rho_{TU}}^2 = \frac{.001281 - .59^2(.75^2)(.525^2).0025 + .75^2(.525^2).0025 + .75^2(.75^2).0090}{(.75^2)(.75^2)(.525^2)}$$

$$= \frac{.001281 - .001261}{.087209} = .000229$$

Thus for the desired true score population correlation distribution, we come up with $\bar{\rho} = .59$ and $\sigma_\rho = .015$, which is very close to the $\bar{\rho} = .60$ and $\sigma_\rho = .00$ actually used to construct the table.

PERSONNEL SELECTION RESEARCH: FIXED TEST

Personnel selection is a special case because in the practical application, the predictor test is used in imperfect form. Thus the relevant population correlation is corrected for error of

TABLE 3.7 Cumulative Analysis of Personnel Selection

Selection Ratio	u	Criterion Reliability	Sample Size	Observed Correlation	b	c
.20	.468	.80	68	.35**	.894	.529
.20	.468	.60	68	.07	.775	.529
.20	.468	.80	68	.11	.894	.529
.20	.468	.60	68	.31*	.775	.529
.50	.603	.80	68	.18	.894	.643
.50	.603	.60	68	.36**	.775	.643
.50	.603	.80	68	.40**	.894	.643
.50	.603	.60	68	.13	.775	.643
.90	.844	.80	68	.49**	.894	.857
.90	.844	.60	68	.23	.775	.857
.90	.844	.80	68	.29*	.894	.857
.90	.844	.60	68	.44*	.775	.857

*p < .05 (2-tailed).
**p < .01 (2-tailed).

measurement in the dependent variable but not the independent variable. Of course in the *theory* of personnel selection, we would want fully corrected correlations as in the previous section.

Personnel selection research is vexed by all four artifacts. Restriction in range on the independent variable is created by selective hiring. However, in personnel selection, it is the test itself that is used to hire and not the test true score. Thus the validity of the test is given by the applicant population correlation between uncorrected test scores and job performance true scores. In local validation studies this would mean that we should correct for error in the job performance measure and correct for restriction in range, but not correct for error of measurement in the test.

If all studies were done with exactly the same test, then a cumulative analysis would be straightforward. We would use the correction formulas of the previous section, substituting 1 for a and 0 for σ_a^2. As an example, we will apply this method to the personnel selection example from Table 3.4 (see Table 3.7).

$$\bar{b} = .8345 \qquad\qquad \bar{c} = .6763 \qquad\qquad \bar{r} = .28$$

$$\sigma_b^2 = .00354 \qquad\qquad \sigma_c^2 = .01849 \qquad\qquad \sigma_r^2 = .01703$$

$$c_i = \sqrt{u^2 + (1 - u^2)\bar{r}^2} \qquad\qquad \sigma_e^2 = .01249$$

$$\sigma_{\rho_{xy}}^2 = .00454$$

$$\bar{\rho}_{xU} = \frac{.28}{(.8345)(.6763)} = .496$$

$$\bar{\rho}_{xU} = .50$$

$$\sigma_{\rho_{xU}}^2 = \frac{\sigma_{\rho_{xy}}^2 - \bar{\rho}_{xU}^2 (\bar{b}^2 \, \sigma_c^2 + \bar{c} \, \sigma_b^2)}{\bar{b}^2 \, \bar{c}^2}$$

$$= \frac{.00454 - (.50)^2 [(.8345)^2 (.01849) + (.6763)^2 (.00354)]}{(.8345)^2 (.6763)^2}$$

$$= \frac{.00454 - .00362}{.31852}$$

$$= \frac{.00092}{.31852}$$

$$\sigma_{\rho_{xU}}^2 = .00287$$

$$SD_{\rho_{xU}} = .05$$

The final estimates are thus $\bar{\rho} = .50$ and $SD_\rho = .05$. The mean value of .50 is exactly correct and the SD_ρ estimate is not much different from the correct value of zero. These estimates can be compared with those obtained in Table 3.5 when for the same data each correlation was corrected individually. Those values were $\bar{\rho} = .49$ and $SD_\rho = 0$. The individual correction leads to the correct conclusion $\sigma_\rho = 0$, while correction using distributions lead to

σ_p = .05, which implies the existence of variation that is not really there. However, a standard deviation of .05 relative to a mean of .50 is only a small variation and would not lead to any difference in practice within personnel selection.

PERSONNEL SELECTION RESEARCH: VARYING TESTS

The test used for prediction is usually only specified in terms of the variable to be measured; for example, arithmetic reasoning. There are many arithmetic reasoning tests available, all of which are equivalent in general content, but different in reliability. This variation in reliability contributes to the variation in correlations across studies if the review covers all studies using a given predictor rather than a fixed test.

There have been two responses to this in the literature. In our earlier work, we ignored variation in the reliability of the predictor (as did Callender and Osburn [1980]). In our recent work, we have used a hybrid solution. We correct the variance across studies for all artifacts; i.e., we use a formula similar to that derived from the quadruple-product equation above. However, we correct the mean only for restriction in range and for error of measurement in job performance. This gives the parameters for a distribution of validities in which the reliability of the predictor is always fixed at the average value for the study population. If the results are to be applied in a context in which the actual test used has a reliability equal to the average reliability, then our results can be used as is. However, if the results are to be used in a context in which the reliability is different from the average, then the user must modify our numbers. The mean validity must first be corrected for attenuation using the mean test reliability, and then that validity must be attenuated using the reliability of the actual test to be used.

**PERSONNEL SELECTION RESEARCH:
ACTUAL FORMULAS IN THE LITERATURE**

The formulas presented above are the simplest formulas yet presented for personnel research. This is because the present formulas drop all terms from the product variance that involve the product of two or more variances. The actual formulas developed in the literature differ from one another in introducing one or more of these terms into the approximation. These terms are trivial in magnitude and hence make little contribution to the quality of the approximation. However, the added terms do make different formulas and hence lead to Monte Carlo studies to see which one is "best" (see, for example, Callender & Osburn, 1980). These studies have found only trivial differences that would be expected from the minute size of the product terms involved. The formulas are presented below for comparison purposes:

Our noninteractive formula (Pearlman et al., 1980):

$$\sigma^2_{\rho_{xU}} = \frac{(\sigma^2_r - \sigma^2_e) - \bar{\rho}^2_{TU}(\sigma^2_b + \bar{b}^2 \sigma^2_a + \bar{b}^2 \bar{a}^2 \sigma^2_c)}{\bar{b}^2 \bar{c}^2}$$

Our "interactive" formula (Schmidt, Gast-Rosenberg, & Hunter, 1980):

$$\sigma^2_{\rho_{xU}} = \frac{(\sigma^2_r - \sigma^2_e) - \bar{\rho}^2_{TU} \sigma^2_{abc}}{\bar{b}^2 \bar{c}^2}$$

The Callender and Osburn (1980) formula:

$$\sigma^2_{\rho_{xU}} = \frac{(\sigma^2_r - \sigma^2_e) - \bar{\rho}^2_{xU}(\bar{c}^2 \sigma^2_b + \bar{b}^2 \sigma^2_c + \sigma^2_b \sigma^2_c)}{(\bar{b}^2 + \sigma^2_b)(\bar{c}^2 + \sigma^2_c)}$$

SUMMARY OF META-ANALYSIS TO CUMULATE CORRELATIONS ACROSS STUDIES

Correlations are subject to three artifactual sources of variation that we can control in a meta-analysis: sampling error, error of measurement, and range variation. Sampling error and error of measurement are found in every study and hence a full meta-analysis should always correct for both. The only exceptions would be in research areas in which there is no published data on the reliability of the measures used. Some domains are not subject to significant amounts of range variation across studies, but in areas with high degrees of subject selection such as personnel selection research, the effects of range restriction can be as large as the effects of error of measurement.

All meta-analyses can be corrected for sampling error. We need only know the sample size N_i for each correlation r_i. The mean and variance of observed sample correlations are used to estimate the mean and variance of population correlations as follows:

$$\bar{\rho}_{xy} = \bar{r}_{xy}$$

$$\sigma^2_{\rho_{xy}} = \sigma^2_{r_{xy}} - \sigma^2_e$$

where σ^2_e is the sampling error variance. However, in this analysis, the correlations analyzed are the correlations between imperfectly measured variables (which are thus systematically lowered by error of measurement) as computed on observed rather than reference populations (so that these correlations are not corrected for range variation). Thus the mean correlation $\bar{\rho}_{xy}$ is a biased estimate of the desired mean correlation $\bar{\rho}_{TU}$ between perfectly measured variables, and it is computed on the wrong population if there is range variation. Furthermore, the corrected variance $\sigma^2_{\rho_{xy}}$ is still biased upward because it contains variance due to differences in reliability across studies and variance due to differences in range (if any).

The effects of error of measurement can be eliminated from the meta-analysis in either of two ways. If reliability information is available on each study, then each correlation is separately corrected for attentuation and the corrected correlations are subjected to meta-analysis to eliminate sampling error. If reliability information is only sporadically available, then the reliability distributions can be used to correct the variance of the uncorrected correlations. If distributions are used, then we proceed in two steps: (1) the variance of observed correlations is corrected for sampling error and (2) the mean and corrected variances are then corrected for the effects of error of measurement using the distribution information on reliabilities.

In a context in which range variation is important, the effects of artifacts can be eliminated in either of two ways. If reliability information and range information are available on each study, then we correct each study correlation for attenuation and range departure. These corrected correlations are then subjected to meta-analysis to eliminate the effect of sampling error. If reliability and range information are only available sporadically, then we use distribution formulas for the meta-analysis. That is, we first correct the variance of observed correlations for sampling error, and then correct the mean and corrected variance for error of measurement and range variation using the distributional formulas.

If the fully corrected variance of correlations across studies suggests that there is a moderator variable, then appropriate candidate variables can be checked by analyzing subsets of studies. If distributional formulas are used on subsets, then only the observed correlations would be averaged within subsets. The artifact distributions for the overall set of studies would still be used within subsets. It is a rare data set that would provide enough artifact values to estimate distributions within subsets.

4

Cumulation Formulas for Effect Sizes

☐ In this chapter we present the cumulation formulas for experimental effects. For simplicity we consider only the case of dichotomous comparisons such as experimental group versus control group. Such data could be analyzed correlationally. The size of the treatment effect could be measured by the (point-biserial) correlation between treatment and effect. This correlation would have the advantage of lending itself to multivariate techniques such as partial correlation, multiple regression, and path analysis. However, most meta-analysts have chosen to use a measure of effect size called "d"; the difference between the group means divided by the standard deviation. It matters little since either statistic can be algebraically transformed into the other.

The d statistic is affected by all the same artifacts as the correlation, including sampling error, error of measurement, and range variation, but the terminology is the same only for sampling error. Many experimenters believe that error of measurement is irrelevant in experiments since it averages out in the group means. However, error of measurement enters the variance of the dependent variable and hence enters the denominator of d. Thus the value of d is systematically lowered by error of measurement, and differences across studies in the reliability of the dependent variable produce spurious differences in the value of d.

Error of measurement in the independent variable is not acknowledged by most experimenters. In their own mind, they believe that persons are unequivocally assigned to one treatment group or the other. But those who have used manipulation checks have found that what is nominally the same treatment for all may be a very different thing to different persons. Some hear the instructions while some do not. Some give one meaning to ambiguous instructions while others give another. We too will ignore error of measurement in the independent variable, but that does not mean that it is not there.

Range variation goes under another name in experimental work, namely, "strength of treatment." In dichotomous experiments, the independent variable is scored 0-1, regardless of how strong the treatment effect is. However, if differences in treatments across studies can be coded, then treatment effects can be projected to a common reference strength and the results of different studies become comparable.

Our coverage of d will focus primarily on sampling error. In most domains there will be no studies that report the reliability of the dependent variable, and hence there will be no possibility of correcting for attenuation. In most domains, there is no measurement of treatment strength, and hence it is not possible to correct studies to a comparable value. However, in a meta-analysis, it might be possible to scale treatment strengths after the fact. In this case, one could either use the correction procedure given here or treat the scaled treatment strength as a moderator variable to see how well it works.

EFFECT SIZE: t, r, AND d

Consider an intervention such as training managers in interpersonal skills. The effect of such an intervention might be assessed by comparing the performance of managers who have had such training (the experimental group) with performance of comparable managers who have not (the control group). The usual comparison statistic is t (or F, which in this context is just the square of t, i.e., $F = t^2$). However, this is a very poor statistic since its size depends on the amount of sampling error in the data. The optimal statistic (which measures size of effect in a metric suitable for path analysis of covariance or other effects) is the point-biserial correlation r. The great advantage of the point-biserial correlation is that it can be inserted into a correlation matrix in which the intervention is then treated like any other variable. For example, the partial correlation between the intervention and the dependent variable with some prior individual difference variable held constant is equivalent to the corresponding analysis of covariance. Path analysis can be used to trace out the difference between direct and indirect effects of the intervention. For example, training might enhance the interpersonal skills of supervisors. This in turn might increase their subordinates' satisfaction with the supervisor, which then might cause a decrease in subordinate absenteeism. If this is the case, then path analysis would show the training to have a direct effect only on the supervisors' interpersonal skills, even though the intervention was also having second-order and third-order indirect effects on subordinate satisfaction and absenteeism, respectively. The theory of sampling error for the point-biserial correlation is identical to the theory for the Pearson correlation given in the previous section, except that the point-biserial correlation may need to be corrected for unequal sample sizes before cumulation (as discussed below).

Glass (1978) and his associates have popularized a transform of the point-biserial correlation called the effect size. The effect size is the difference between the means in standard score form, i.e., the ratio of the difference between the means to the standard deviation. The two variants of the effect size statistic are determined by considering two different standard deviations that might be used for the denominator. The standard deviation that will be used here is the within-group standard deviation of analysis of variance. The alternative is the control-group standard deviation as used by Smith and Glass (1977). However, since there is rarely a large difference between the control and experimental group (a comparison that can be separately cumulated), it seems reasonable to use the statistic with the least sampling error. The within-group standard deviation has only about half the sampling error of the control-group standard deviation.

If the variance for the experimental group is s_E^2 and the variance for the control group is s_C^2, then the within-group variance s^2 is defined by

$$s^2 = \frac{(N_E - 1) s_E^2 + (N_C - 1) s_C^2}{N_E + N_C - 2}$$

The effect-size statistic d is then defined by

$$d = \frac{\bar{y}_E - \bar{y}_C}{s}$$

That is, d is the difference between the means divided by the within-group standard deviation.

The three statistics d, t, and r are all algebraically transformable from one to the other. These transformations will be shown below for the special case of equal sample sizes in the two groups, i.e., for $N_E = N_C = N/2$ where N is the total sample size for that study.

$$d = \frac{2}{\sqrt{N}} \qquad t = \sqrt{\frac{N-2}{N}} \; \frac{2r}{\sqrt{1-r^2}}$$

For small correlations, this means d = 2r or r = d/2

$$t = \frac{\sqrt{N}}{2} \qquad d = \sqrt{N-2} \; \frac{r}{\sqrt{1-r^2}}$$

$$r = \frac{t}{\sqrt{t^2 + N - 2}} = \frac{d}{\sqrt{d^2 + \dfrac{4(N-2)}{N}}}$$

Some studies characterize the outcome in statistics other than t, d, or r. Glass, McGaw, and Smith (1981) provide transformation formulas for many such cases. However, the transformed value in such cases will not have the sampling error given by our formulas. In particular probit transformations yield effect sizes with much larger sampling errors than does our formula for d.

CORRECTION FOR UNEQUAL SAMPLE SIZE

Conceptually, the effect size is normally thought of independently of the sample sizes of the control and experimental groups. However, in a natural environment, the importance of a difference depends on how often it occurs. Thus the relative frequency of the two conditions enters the correlation coefficient. If the two sample sizes are discrepant, then the point-biserial correlation should be corrected to what it would be for equal sample sizes. The formula for this correction is

$$r_c = \frac{r}{\sqrt{4pq(1 - r^2) + r^2}}$$

where

$$pq = \frac{N_E N_C}{N^2}$$

The effect size is already expressed independently of the two sample sizes, though that poses certain problems for natural groups of quite uneven sizes (such as persons with and without migraine).

AN ALTERNATIVE TO d

Glass has often used a variation on the d statistic. He uses the control-group standard deviation instead of the within-group standard deviation. His reason for this is that the treatment may have an effect on the experimental-group standard deviation as well as on the experimental group mean. That point is well taken;

where there is a treatment effect, there may well be a treatment by subject interaction. However, if we wish to check for this, there is a much more effective procedure than altering the definition of d. We do a meta-analysis that compares the values of the standard deviations directly.

Let the statistic v be defined by

$$v = \frac{s_E}{s_C}$$

That is, let v be the ratio of the experimental-group standard deviation to the control-group standard deviation. If the meta-analysis shows up a value other than 1, then we will have shown the existence of a treatment by subject interaction and we will have an inkling as to its nature.

Let us use the symbol d_G to denote the Glass variation on the effect size d. That is, let us define the symbol d_G by

$$d_G = \frac{\bar{y}_E - \bar{y}_C}{s_C}$$

If the meta-analysis shows the value of v to be 1, then the population values of d and d_G are the same. If the meta-analysis shows the value of v to be other than 1, then the meta-analysis value for d can be transformed into the meta-analysis value of d_G by the following identity:

$$d_G = d \sqrt{\frac{1 + v^2}{2}}$$

Deadline pressures prevent our derivation of the sampling error variance formula required for the meta-analysis of v at this time. However, this formula will probably be available from the senior author by the time this book is published.

There are two principle advantages to using the within-group standard deviation rather than the control-group standard deviation, i.e., using d rather than d_G. First, the control-group standard deviation (and hence d_G) has much more sampling error than does the within-group standard deviation (and hence d). Second, most reports have a value for t or F and hence permit the computation of d. Few reports present standard deviations in which case d_G cannot be computed. Therefore we have chosen to develop and present meta-analysis formulas only for d.

SAMPLING ERROR IN d

Let us denote the population value of the effect size statistic by δ. The observed value d will then deviate from δ by sampling error. We will use the large sample approximations

$$E(d) = \delta$$

$$\sigma_e^2 = \frac{4}{N}\left(1 + \frac{\delta^2}{8}\right)$$

Exact formulas can be found in Hedges (1980, p. 42). (However, the large sample formula in Corrolary 3.1 on page 43 is in error. Because of a typo, the $2/m_i$ in his variance formula should be $4/m_i$. Hedges's formula can be simplified by eliminating the gamma functions. In his notation, the crucial very close approximation is $c(m) = (4m - 7)/(4m - 4)$.)

CUMULATION AND CORRECTION OF
THE VARIANCE FOR SAMPLING ERROR

The basic cumulation process is the same for effect sizes as for correlations: Compute the frequency weighted mean and variance of the effect size over studies, then correct the variance for sampling error. The formulas follow:

$$\bar{d} = \frac{\Sigma[N_i d_i]}{\Sigma N_i}$$

$$\sigma_d^2 = \frac{\Sigma[N_i(d_i - \bar{d})^2]}{\Sigma N_i}$$

$$\sigma_e^2 = \frac{\Sigma\left[N_i 4/N_i \left(1 + \frac{\bar{d}^2}{8}\right)\right]}{\Sigma N_i} = \frac{4(1 + \bar{d}^2/8)K}{N}$$

where K is the number of studies and N is the total sample size across studies. The variance of effect size corrected for sampling error is

$$\sigma_\delta^2 = \sigma_d^2 - \sigma_e^2$$

Thus if the observed distribution is characterized by the values $\bar{d}$ and σ_d, then the actual distribution of effect sizes is characterized by $\bar{\delta}$ and σ_δ where

$$\bar{\delta} = \bar{d}$$

$$\sigma_\delta = \sqrt{\sigma_d^2 - \sigma_e^2}$$

For example, given the values

N	d
100	−.01
90	.41*
50	.50*
40	−.10

(*Significant at the .05 level.)

we have

$$\bar{d} = \frac{100(-.01) + 90(.41) + 50(.50) + 40(-.10)}{100 + 90 + 50 + 40}$$

$$= \frac{56.9}{280} = .20$$

$$\sigma_d^2 = \frac{100(-.01 - .20)^2 + 90(.41 - .20)^2 + 50(.50 - .20)^2 + \ldots}{100 + 90 + 50 + 40}$$

$$= \frac{16.479}{280} = .0589$$

$$\sigma_e^2 = \frac{4(1 + \bar{d}^2/8)K}{N} = \frac{4(1 + .20^2/8)4}{280} = \frac{16.08}{280} = .0574$$

$$\sigma_\delta^2 = \sigma_d^2 - \sigma_e^2 = .0589 - .0574 = .0015$$

and hence

$$\bar{\delta} = .20$$

$$\sigma_\delta = .04$$

If the effect size is really the same across studies, then σ_δ will be approximately 0. Even if there is some variation across studies, the value for σ_δ may still be small enough to ignore for practical or theoretical reasons. If the variation is large, especially if it is large relative to the mean value, then there should be a search for moderator variables.

AN EXAMPLE: LEADERSHIP TRAINING BY EXPERTS

Organizational psychologists have long suspected that training in interpersonal or leadership skills improves the performance of managers. Professor Fruitloop decided that he wanted to know the amount of improvement and therefore laid out the design of a cumulative study. He decided that studies should meet two criteria. First, each training program must contain at

TABLE 4.1 Leadership Training

Author	Sample Size	Effect Size
Apple	40	-.24
Banana	40	-.04
Cherry	40	.20
Orange	40	.44*
Melon	40	.64*

*Significant at the .05 level.

least three key skills: active listening, negative feedback, and positive feedback. Second, the study should be run under controlled training conditions. To assure this he used only studies in which the training was done by outside experts (see Table 4.1).

Of the five studies, only two show significant effects. Two of the studies show effects in the opposite direction. Thus, using normal review standards, Fruitloop would be lead to conclude that training in interpersonal skills had no impact (or uncertain impact) on performance of supervisors. But fortunately Fruitloop had heard of cumulation.

$$\bar{d} = .20$$

$$\sigma_d^2 = .1005$$

$$\sigma_e^2 = \frac{4(1 + .20^2/8)5}{200} = .1005$$

$$\sigma_\delta^2 = \sigma_d^2 - \sigma_e^2 = .1005 - .1005 = 0$$

Thus Fruitloop discovered that all the variation in observed results was actually due to sampling error. Thus the studies collected actually showed perfect consistency in the effect of training, though the actual (average) level is much lower than the largest levels found in isolated studies.

MODERATOR VARIABLES AND EFFECT SIZES

The impact of an intervention might vary from setting to setting. For example, training programs might vary in quality, quantity, or in the average learning ability of the trainees. If this were so, then the cumulation formulas would yield nonzero variance for the population effect sizes, i.e., a nonzero value for σ_δ^2. The search for and detection of the moderator variables that account for such variation is then identical to the procedure followed in looking for moderator variables in correlational studies. Indeed, the general mathematics is identical for both. Such searches are highly prone to capitalization on chance unless there are a very large number of studies. There are two ways to see if a study characteristic is a moderator variable or not: Use the characteristic to break the data into subsets or correlate the study characteristic with effect size.

If the data are broken into subsets, then there are two ways that a moderator variable would show itself. First, there should be large differences in the mean effect size between subsets. Second, there should be a reduction in variance within subsets. These are not independent events. We know from analysis of variance that the total variance in effect size is the sum of the variance in mean effect sizes between subsets plus the average within-subset variance. This theorem applies equally well to either observed effect sizes or to population effect sizes. If the usual formula for components of variance is applied to the corrected variances rather than to uncorrected variances, then the result is a value for η_δ^2 instead of η_d^2. This correction of η^2 for sampling error is comparable to correcting the usual within experiment η^2 for error of measurement.

If effect size is correlated with a study characteristic, then the correlation will be attenuated by the sampling error in the observed effect size in the same manner that the ordinary correlations across persons are attenuated by error of measurement. Thus study characteristic correlations should be corrected for sampling error. To do this we define a reliability such as number "Rel(d)" and then use it to correct the observed correlation "Cor(d,y)," where y is the study characteristic.

$$\text{Rel}(d) = \frac{\sigma_\delta^2}{\sigma_d^2} = \frac{\sigma_d^2 - \sigma_e^2}{\sigma_d^2}$$

$$\text{Cor}(\delta,y) = \frac{\text{Cor}(d,y)}{\sqrt{\text{Rel}(d)}}$$

To the extent that the relationship between the study characteristic and effect size is linear, this corrected correlation will be equal to the corrected η obtained using breakdown into subsets.

AN EXAMPLE: TRAINING BY EXPERTS VERSUS TRAINING BY MANAGERS

Jim Russell (personal communication) believes that training of supervisors in interpersonal skills should be done by their own managers rather than by outside experts. He believes that since managers act as role models for the supervisors, the supervisors are much more likely to identify with procedures recommended by managers than with those recommended by outside experts.

Consider again the hypothetical cumulative study done by Fruitloop. Fruitloop discarded all studies done by managers as "lacking in experimental control." Suppose that all studies were analyzed. The results might look like those displayed in Table 4.2.

$$\bar{d} = .30$$

$$\sigma_d^2 = .1105$$

$$\sigma_e^2 = .1013$$

$$\sigma_\delta^2 = .1105 - .1013 = .0092$$

$$\sigma_\delta = .10$$

TABLE 4.2 Training in Interpersonal Skills
(by managers versus by experts)

Author	Trainer	Sample Size	Effect Size
Apple	Expert	40	−.24
Banana	Expert	40	−.04
Cherry	Expert	40	.20
Orange	Expert	40	.44*
Melon	Expert	40	.64*
Cucumber	Manager	40	−.04
Tomato	Manager	40	.16
Squash	Manager	40	.40
Carrot	Manager	40	.64*
Pepper	Manager	40	.84

*Significant at the .05 level.

In this collection of studies, only four of ten have significant effects, though only three of ten go in the opposite direction. Thus normal review practice would still conclude that the effect of training in interpersonal skills is problematic. In fact, the cumulation shows that most of this variation is due to sampling error. A 95 percent confidence interval for δ would go from .10 to .50, which does not include 0. Thus cumulative analysis shows that training always has a positive effect. However, in this case the analysis shows that there is evidence of variation in the size of the effect. This variation could be due to other study artifacts such as reporting error or it could be due to a real moderator variable.

Expert Training

$$\bar{d} = .20$$

$$\sigma_d^2 = .1005$$

$$\sigma_e^2 = .1005$$

$$\sigma_\delta^2 = .1005 - .1005 = 0$$

$$\sigma_\delta = 0$$

Manager Training

$$\bar{d} = .40$$

$$\sigma_d^2 = .1005$$

$$\sigma_e^2 = .1020$$

$$\sigma_\delta^2 = .1005 - .1020 = -.0015$$

$$\sigma_\delta = 0$$

TABLE 4.3 Training in Interpersonal Skills (by hours)

Number Hours	Sample Size	Effect Size
2	40	−.27
2	40	.47*
2	40	.37
2	40	−.17
3	40	−.22
3	40	−.12
3	40	.42
3	40	.52*
4	40	−.17
4	40	.57*
4	40	.47*
4	40	−.07

*Significant at the .05 level.

In our example, breaking studies down by type of trainer eliminates all variation in effect size (other than sampling error). Thus
training by outside experts always has an effect of .20 standard
deviations, while training by managers always has an effect of
twice that size, .40 standard deviations.

ANOTHER EXAMPLE: AMOUNT OF TRAINING

We will now present an example in which the impact of
training on interpersonal skills varies as a function of the number
of hours of training (see Table 4.3). The measure of number of
hours is the amount of time that the trainee is in actual interaction with the trainer (as opposed to watching the trainer work
with someone else).

$$\bar{d} = .15$$

$$\sigma_d^2 = .1066$$

$$\sigma_e^2 = \frac{4(1 + .15^2/8)12}{480} = .1003$$

$$\sigma_\delta^2 = .1066 - .1003 = .0063$$

$$\sigma_\delta = .08$$

In this example, the effect size is significant only four in twelve times and half the studies found effects in the opposite direction. Normal review practice would probably conclude that training in interpersonal skills has no effect. But the cumulative analysis reveals a very different story. The average effect is only .15, but most of the variation is due to sampling error. The 95 percent confidence interval for population effect size is −.01 to .31, which says that training is almost always effective.

2 Hours	3 Hours	4 Hours
$\bar{d} = .10$	$\bar{d} = .15$	$\bar{d} = .20$
$\sigma_d^2 = .1049$	$\sigma_d^2 = .1049$	$\sigma_d^2 = .1049$
$\sigma_e^2 = .1001$	$v_e^2 = .1003$	$\sigma_e^2 = .1005$
$\sigma_\delta^2 = .0048$	$\sigma_\delta^2 = .0046$	$\sigma_\delta^2 = .0044$
$\sigma_\delta = .07$	$\sigma_\delta = .07$	$\sigma_\delta = .07$

$$\eta_{d/II}^2 = \frac{\text{Var}(\bar{d})}{\text{Var}(d)} = \frac{.0017}{.1066} = .0159$$

$$\eta_{d/H} = .13$$

2 Hours	3 Hours	4 Hours
$\bar{\delta} = .10$	$\bar{\delta} = .15$	$\bar{\delta} = .20$
$\sigma_\delta = .07$	$\sigma_\delta = .07$	$\sigma_\delta = .07$

$$\eta_{\delta/H}^2 = \frac{\text{Var}(\bar{\delta})}{\text{Var}(\delta)} = \frac{.0017}{.0063} = .2698$$

$$\eta_{\delta/H} = .52$$

The corresponding correlational analysis is:

$$Cor(d,H) = .13$$

$$Rel(d) = \frac{Var(\delta)}{Var(d)} = \frac{.0063}{.1066} = .0591$$

$$Cor(\delta,H) = \frac{Cor(d,H)}{\sqrt{Rel(d)}} = \frac{.13}{.24} = .54$$

This new analysis shows that effect size depends on the amount of training. Confidence intervals show that effect size is as low as 0 only in the 2-hour training studies. In this example, there is still variation in effect size after one moderator variable has been found. This residual variance could either be due to artifacts such as variation in the quality of performance measurement or due to some other real moderator variable.

CORRECTING EFFECT SIZE ESTIMATES FOR UNRELIABILITY (MEASUREMENT ERROR)

As we stated earlier, less-than-perfect reliability in measuring scales causes correlations to be suppressed from their true score levels. The same is true for the d statistic. Up until now in our discussion of procedures for cumulating effect sizes across studies, we have proceeded as if the observed value $d = (X_e - X_c)/s$ is the effect size value of interest. Actually, to the extent that the measurement of the dependent variable is less than perfectly reliable, errors of measurement will cause the observed d value to be an underestimate of the actual effect size. Why this is so can be seen from the fact that the effect of error of measurement is to artifically increase the denominator in the formula for d. To see this, write the observed score X in terms of true score T and error of measurement E, i.e.,

$$X = T + E$$

The population mean of X is unaffected by such error:

$$\mu_X = \mu_T$$

However, the variance is very much affected:

$$\sigma_X^2 = \sigma_T^2 + \sigma_E^2$$

The real effect size is the effect size for true scores. The mean difference in the numerator has no systematic bias due to measurement error, but the denominator does. The correction can be done with the following ratio:

$$d_T = \frac{\bar{X}_E - \bar{X}_C}{S_T} = \frac{\bar{X}_E - \bar{X}_C}{S_X} \cdot \frac{S_X}{S_T}$$

$$= d_X \left(\frac{S_T}{S_X}\right)^{-1}$$

The reliability of X is $r_{XX} = \sigma_T^2 / \sigma_X^2$. Therefore the ratio S_T / S_X is equal to the square root of the reliability (to within sampling error). Hence the desired effect size is

$$d_T = d_X (r_{XX})^{-\frac{1}{2}} = \frac{d_X}{\sqrt{r_{XX}}}$$

The value d can and should be corrected for the attenuating effects of measurement error in exactly the same way as the correlation coefficient. For example, if d is 1.2 and r_{xx} is .60, the best estimate of the true effect size is $1.2/\sqrt{.60} = 1.55$.

If there is variation across studies in the reliability of measures of dependent variables, this fact will cause variation in observed d values (beyond the variation due to sampling error). This variation can be eliminated by correcting observed d values for unreliability. Just as in the case of correlation coefficients (discussed in Chapter 3), the formulas for sampling error have to be modified to take into account the effect of the corrections on sampling error. The formula for error variance is obtained by multiplying the variance for uncorrected d values by the square of the correction factor, i.e., by the reciprocal of the reliability:

$$\sigma_e^2 = \frac{\sum N_i \left(\dfrac{1}{r_{x x_i}}\right) \dfrac{4\left(1 + \dfrac{\bar{d}^2}{8}\right)}{N_i}}{\sum N_i}$$

$$= \frac{4\left(1 + \dfrac{\bar{d}^2}{8}\right) \sum\limits_i \dfrac{1}{r_{x x_i}}}{N}$$

$$= \frac{4\left(1 + \dfrac{\bar{d}^2}{8}\right) K}{N} \cdot \left(\frac{1}{K} \sum \frac{1}{r_{x_i x_i}}\right)$$

The last factor $(1/K) \sum 1/r_{x_i x_i}$ is the average of the reciprocals of the reliabilities. If the reliabilities do not vary much from study to study, then the average of the reciprocals would be approximately the reciprocal of the average. In this case,

$$\sigma_e^2 \approx \frac{1}{\bar{r}_{xx}} \frac{4\left(1 + \dfrac{\bar{d}^2}{8}\right) K}{N}$$

AN EXAMPLE: THE EFFICIENCY OF JOB KNOWLEDGE TRAINING

Alex Lernmor, a psychologist at New York University, developed a new method of training dopplegaggers in the facts they need to operate the machinery on their jobs. His training program has been adopted by many firms in the Northeast that employ dopplegaggers. So far, eight studies have been done in these firms to evaluate the effectiveness of the program. Only three of these studies have been done by Lernmor, but the same

100-item measure of job knowledge was used in all eight studies. In all cases, there were twenty people in the trained group and twenty in the control group (see Table 4.4). Alphonso Kopikat of the University of Texas learned about this program and, in connection with his consulting work, introduced it into many Texas businesses employing dopplegaggers. Seven studies evaluating the method have now been completed in Texas. These studies are much the same as the earlier ones, although to save time, a short 12-item measure of job knowledge was used instead of the lengthy 100-item scale of Lernmor. The results for this set of studies are also shown in Table 4.4.

Lernmor and Kopikat each conducted their own cumulative analysis of these findings. Kopikat had not heard of the attenuating effects of unreliability on effect size estimates and therefore conducted his analysis on observed values of d. Here are his results:

$$\bar{d}_x = .782$$

$$\sigma^2_{d_x} = .18044$$

$$\sigma^2_e = .10765$$

$$\sigma^2_\delta = .18044 - .10765 = .07279$$

$$\sigma_\delta = .27$$

95 percent Confidence Interval = .25 – 1.31
Observed Variance Accounted for = .10765/.18044 = 59.6 percent

Kopikat concluded that the mean effect size was .78 but that the effect size could go as low as .25, which he did not think was very impressive. He noted that after the effects of sampling error were removed, 40 percent of the variance still remained. This led him to suspect that moderator variables were operating. The one he suspected most strongly was geographical location. He had heard that Texans were slower learners than Northerners and so he hypothesized that while the program would work in Texas, it would not work as well as it did in the Northeast. His hunch apparently paid off, for when he calculated the effect sizes

TABLE 4.4 Efficiency of Job Knowledge Training

Study	Location	Sample Size	Observed Effect Size (d_x)	Reliability of Scale	Estimated True Effect Size (d_T)
1	NE	40	.66*	.90	.69
2	NE	40	1.74**	.90	1.84
3	NE	40	1.61**	.90	1.70
4	NE	40	.89**	.90	.94
5	NE	40	.39ns	.90	.41
6	NE	40	.47ns	.90	.49
7	NE	40	.77*	.90	.81
8	NE	40	.71*	.90	.75
9	Texas	40	.90**	.50	1.27
10	Texas	40	.44ns	.50	.62
11	Texas	40	.32ns	.50	.45
12	Texas	40	1.16**	.50	1.64
13	Texas	40	.58**	.50	.81
14	Texas	40	.86**	.50	1.21
15	Texas	40	.25ns	.50	.36

*Significant at the .05 level.
**Significant at the .01 level.

separately by region, the mean effect size was .90 for the Northeast but only .64 for Texas. He concluded that the training program was about 30 percent less effective in Texas. His confidence in his findings was further bolstered when he found that both σ_d^2 and σ_ε^2 were smaller within regions than had been the case for this overall analysis (although we will forego presenting these figures here). Kopikat's study was widely acclaimed as yet another convincing demonstration of the importance of moderator variables when it was published in the *Statistical Artifact Review* (1975, 66, 398-447).

Having read the very book you are now reading, Lernmor was aware of the attenuating effects of measurement error on estimates of effect size. He determined that the 12-item job knowledge scale used in the Texas studies had a reliability of only .50. He had previously shown that his long measure was quite reliable (.90). Before conducting his analysis, Lernmor corrected for attenuation using the formula given above. With such large differences in reliability across studies, the approximation for the error variance could not be used. Here are his results:

$$\bar{d}_T = .933$$

$$\sigma^2_{d_T} = .22370$$

$$\sigma^2_e = .16426$$

$$\sigma^2_\delta = .22370 - .16426 = .05944$$

$$\sigma_\delta = .24$$

95% Confidence Interval = .46 – 1.40
Observed Variance Accounted for = .16426/.22370 = 73.4 percent

Thus Lernmor concluded that the mean effect size was .933, almost 20 percent larger than Kopikat had concluded it to be. Furthermore, Lernmor's minimum value of .46 is almost twice as large as Kopikat's minimum value of .25. Thus the correct analysis showed that Kopikat had substantially underestimated the effectiveness of Lernmor's training program.

Lernmor was also concerned about Kopikat's report that the program was less effective in some parts of the country. Lernmor noted that reliability differences and sampling error accounted for almost three-fourths of the variation across studies, which did not leave much room for moderator variables to operate. Nevertheless, he looked at the mean corrected effect size separately for Texas and the Northeast. For Texas, d_T was .91 and for Northeast, it was .95. There was no moderator effect. Hence his correct analysis not only avoided underestimating the effectiveness of the program, as the incorrect analysis had done; it also showed that Kopikat's moderator effect was an artifact created by his failure to take into account study differences in measurement reliability.

5
Cumulation of Results Within Studies

☐ It is often possible to obtain more than one correlation or estimate of effect size from within the same study. Should these estimates be contributed as independent estimates? Or should there be some cumulation within the study so that only one value is contributed? There is no one answer to these questions since there are several different kinds of replication that can take place within studies. This chapter surveys the cases that are most frequent.

Many single studies have replication of observation of a relationship within the study. Thus there can be cumulation of results within, as well as across, studies. However, the method of cumulation depends on the nature of the replication process used in the study. Three kinds of replication will be considered here: fully replicated designs, conceptual replication, and analysis of subgroups.

FULLY REPLICATED DESIGNS

A fully replicated design occurs in a study if that study can be broken into parts that are conceptually equivalent but statistically independent. For example, if data are gathered at several different organizations, then statistics calculated within organizations can be regarded as replicated across organizations. The outcome measures from each organization are statistically independent and can be treated as if they were values from different studies. That is, the cumulation process for these values is the same as that for cumulation across studies. The correction for sampling error displays the true degree of variation across organizations (unless some of the other artifacts are present) and hence the true extent of moderation in the relationship due to organizations.

CONCEPTUAL REPLICATION

Conceptual replication occurs within a study when more than one observation that is relevant to a given relationship is made on each subject. The most common example is replicated measurement, the use of multiple indicators to assess a given variable. For example, the use of several items to assess skill variety; the use of training grades, selection test scores, and job knowledge tests to assess cognitive ability for work performance; or the use of peer ratings, supervisor ratings, and production records to assess job performance. The second most common example is observation in multiple situations. For example, a participant in an assessment center may be asked to show problem solving skills in Task A, Task B, and so on. The observations in the various situations can be regarded as replicated measurements of problem-solving skill.

The replication within the study can be used in either of two ways: (1) Each conceptual replication can be represented by a different outcome value, and these separate outcome values can either be cumulated within the study or contributed as a set to a larger cumulation, or (2) the measurements can be combined using confirmatory factor analysis, and the resulting single-outcome measure can be used to assess the relationship in question.

MULTIPLE OUTCOME VALUES WITHIN A STUDY

Suppose that three variables are used as indicators of job performance: peer rating, supervisor rating, and a job sample test. Any potential selection test could then have three correlations that are conceptually all validity coefficients: the correlation between test and peer rating, the correlation between test and supervisor rating, and the correlation between test and job sample test. These values could contribute to a larger cumulative study in two ways: The three correlations could be contributed as three separate values (the most common approach in contemporary studies) or the three correlations could be averaged and the average could be contributed as the one value representing the study.

If the set of correlations is contributed to the larger study, then there is a problem for the cumulation formulas laid out in Chapter 3. These formulas assume that the values used are statistically independent of each other. This is guaranteed if the values come from different studies, but is only true in the present example if the correlations between peer rating, supervisor rating, and job sample test are all 0 (as population values for that study), which is impossible if the measures are even approximately equivalent as they are believed to be. If the number of values contributed by each study is small in comparison to the number of studies, then there is little error in the resulting cumulation. However, if a very large number of values are contributed from one small study, then there can still be considered distortion if statistical significance tests are used (see, for example, Hunter, Schmidt, & Hunter, 1979; Schmidt, Pearlman, & Hunter, 1980).

If the average correlation is used to represent the study, then there is no violation of the independence assumption. However, what are we to use for the sample size of the average correlation? If we use the total number of observation that go into the average correlation (i.e., the product of sample size times the number of correlations averaged), then we greatly underestimate the sampling error since this assumes that we have averaged independent correlations. On the other hand, if we use the sample size of the study, then we greatly overestimate the sampling error since the average correlation will have less sampling error than a single correlation. The exact sampling error in the average correlation will be made clear in the discussion of composite scores to follow. In most studies, there is much less error in assuming the simple sample size for the average correlation.

There is another potential problem with the average correlation. In those rare cases in which there is a strong moderator variable, i.e., cases in which there is a large, real, corrected standard deviation across studies, the moderator variable may vary within studies as well as across studies. In such a case, the average correlation would be conceptually ambiguous.

CONCEPTUAL REPLICATION AND CONFIRMATORY FACTOR ANALYSIS

Multiple measurements can be used to generate correlations with smaller measurement error or to estimate correlations without measurement error (Hunter & Gerbing, 1982). The crucial question is the extent to which measures believed to be equivalent are in fact measures of the same underlying trait. If the replicated measures are equivalent in the sense of reliability theory, then measurement error can be reduced by using a composite score formed by averaging the standard scores (or by just adding the raw scores if the standard deviations are all about the same). If the correlations for this composite score are corrected for attenuation, then measurement error is eliminated altogether. In the case of the items in a scale, the composite score is the test score and the true score is the factor measured without error.

In confirmatory factor analysis, the same distinction is made in terms of the jargon of factor analysis. If the analysis is done "with ones in the diagonal," then the factor is the composite score. If the analysis is done "with communalities," then the factor is the underlying trait measured without error. If the alternate indicators are equivalent in the sense of reliability theory, i.e., they differ only by random response error, then the computations of confirmatory factor analysis are identical to those of reliability theory. However, confirmatory factor analysis is valid in certain situations in which reliability theory fails. Hunter and Gerbing (1982) note that if the indicator variables define a general factor, and if the specific factors are irrelevant to the other variables being considered, then at the level of second-order factor analysis the indicator variables satisfy the assumptions of reliability theory, and confirmatory factor analysis generates the correct correlation between the general factor that was intended to be measured and the other variable. For example, it is quite likely that peer rating, supervisor rating, and the job sample test each measure specific factors in addition to the general factor of job performance. However, if these specific factors are uncorrelated with each other and with the selection test, then confirmatory factor analysis will generate a correct correlation between the test and job performance. However, in the case of second-order analysis, the correction for attenuation is not made with the reliability of the composite score but with a slightly smaller number. The reliability of the composite would be Mosier's (1943) formula with indicator reliabilities in the numerator diagonal, whereas the equivalent correction formula for second-order analysis is Mosier's formula with communalities in the numerator diagonal. Thus second-order factor analysis correctly treats the specific factors as error.

There is a strong algebraic relationship between the average correlation and the correlation for the composite score. Let the indicator variables be denoted $x_1, x_2, \ldots, x_n$; let the composite score be denoted X; and let the other variable be denoted y. Let $\bar{r}_{xy}$ be the average correlation between the individual indicators and y, i.e., let $\bar{r}_{xy}$ be the average of $r_{x_1 y}$, $r_{x_2 y}$, and so on. Let $\bar{r}_{xx}$ be the average correlation between the indicator variables, i.e., let $\bar{r}_{xx}$ be the average of $r_{x_1 x_2}$, $r_{x_1 x_3}$, $r_{x_2 x_3}$, and so on. Let $\bar{c}_{xx}$ be the average covariance between the indicators, i.e., let $\bar{c}_{xx}$ be defined by

$$\bar{c}_{xx} = \frac{1 + (n-1)\bar{r}_{xx}}{n}$$

Then the relationship between the average correlation $\bar{r}_{xy}$ and the composite score correlation r_{Xy} is given by

$$r_{Xy} = \frac{\bar{r}_{xy}}{\sqrt{\bar{c}_{xx}}}$$

The number $\bar{r}_{xx}$ is a fraction; $0 \leqslant \bar{r}_{xx} \leqslant 1$. The number $\bar{c}_{xx}$ is a weighted average of $\bar{r}_{xx}$ and 1 and hence is between them:

$$0 \leqslant \bar{r}_{xx} \leqslant \bar{c}_{xx} \leqslant 1$$

Since $\bar{c}_{xx}$ is a fraction, its square root is also a fraction and it lies between $\bar{c}_{xx}$ and 1; i.e.,

$$0 \leqslant \bar{r}_{xx} \leqslant \bar{c}_{xx} \leqslant \sqrt{\bar{c}_{xx}} \leqslant 1$$

To divide r_{xx} by a fraction is to increase its size. Thus for positive correlations we have

$$r_{Xy} \geqslant r_{xy}$$

That is, the composite score correlation is always larger in size than the average correlation. It is the composite correlation whose sampling error is given by the conventional formula with the study sample size. The standard error of the average correlation is smaller than that by exactly the multiplicative factor $\sqrt{\bar{c}_{xx}}$. Thus the composite score correlation enters into a larger cumulation in exact accordance with the assumptions about sampling error made by the cumulation formulas in Chapter 3, while the average correlation is off. If the conceptual assumptions of the study are correct, then the composite score correlation is also more accurate numerically.

From a conceptual point of view, the number we really want is the correlation for the composite without measurement error, i.e., the correlation obtained from confirmatory factor analysis with communalities. This number will be larger than the composite score correlation (and hence larger than the average correlation), though often not by much. However, a corrected correlation does not have the same standard error as an uncorrected correlation, but is larger by the same multiplicative factor of correction (as shown earlier). If the correlations are corrected for attenuation or generated using confirmatory factor analysis with communalities, then the cumulative variance should be corrected using the formulas given in Chapter 3.

For example, suppose that peer rating, supervisor rating, and a job sample test were each correlated .60 with each other.

Then

$$\bar{r}_{xx} = .60, \ c_{xx} = .73, \ \sqrt{c_{xx}} = .86$$

and hence

$$r_{Xy} = 1.16 \ \bar{r}_{xy}$$

That is, the composite score correlation would be about 16 percent larger than the average correlation. If T is job performance measured without error, then the trait correlation r_{Ty} is related to the others by

$$r_{Ty} = \frac{r_{Xy}}{\sqrt{r_{XX}}} = 1.10 \ r_{Xy} = 1.28 \ \bar{r}_{xy}$$

where r_{XX} is the "reliability" of the composite score calculated using Mosier's (1943) formula with communalities in the numerator diagonal (which is also equal to coefficient alpha [Cronbach, 1951] calculated using the correlations between the scales). Thus the correlation for actual job performance is 10 percent larger than the composite score correlation, and 28 percent larger than the average correlation.

CONCEPTUAL REPLICATION: CONCLUSION

If a set of indicator variables is statistically as well as psychologically equivalent at either the level of primary or second-order factor analysis, then the ideal cumulation within a study is confirmatory factor analysis with communalities. The composite score correlation is poorer, but usually not by much. The average correlation is usually noticeably poorer. If the set of indicators deviates considerably from the unifactor model, then the set of individual correlations should be contributed to the larger cumulation.

Alas, there is a practical side to this issue. Published studies typically do not currently present whole correlation matrices, but often show only selected correlations. Thus the composite score correlation may not be computable and the confirmatory factor analysis may not be computable. The unifactor hypothesis cannot even be tested for many studies. For such studies, the choice defaults to the use of individual correlations versus the use of the average correlation.

If confirmatory factor analysis is possible, then it has several additional benefits. Baseline correlations are higher because of the elimination of error of measurement. There is a drastic reduction in the size of the study correlation matrix, and hence in the opportunity for capitalization on chance. The drastic reduction in the size of the correlation matrix creates a corresponding and appropriate drastic reduction in the conceptual complexity of any causal model that might fit the data.

ANALYSIS OF SUBGROUPS

For many it has now become routine to analyze data separately by race and sex, even though there is usually no reason to believe that either will act as a moderator. It partly stems from a common confusion between additive and moderator effects. For example, it is widely believed that the technology of an organization sets limits on its managerial philosophy. For example, large-scale manufacturing requires rigid coordination of work and hence provides fewer opportunities for power sharing with subordinates. This leads to the prediction that the level of consideration will be lower in manufacturing organizations. However, within such organizations it may still be true that those who bring workers into their decision-making structure will have higher production. Thus the *correlation* need not be lower in such plants even though the mean is.

If demographic membership is a real and substantial moderator, then the subgroup correlations can be entered into the larger cumulation as independent outcome values. Statistically, outcome values for nonoverlapping groups have the same properties as values from different studies.

SUBGROUPS AND LOSS OF POWER

But the analysis of subgroups exacts a terrible price. Consider an example in which 100 persons are evenly split by race and by sex. There will then be 4 subgroups: 25 black females, 25 black males, 25 white females, and 25 white males. An outcome value for a sample size of 25 has much more sampling error than an outcome based on 100 cases. In fact, the confidence interval for 25 cases is exactly twice as wide as that for 100 cases. For the full sample, an observed correlation of .20 would have a confidence interval of $.00 \leqslant p \leqslant .40$. For a subsample, the confidence interval would be $-.20 \leqslant p \leqslant .60$. There is actually very little information in an observed correlation based on as few as 25 cases (though it can be cumulated with other small-sample correlations and make a contribution in this way).

The immense statistical uncertainty and sampling error in subgroups leads to immense capitalization on chance. For simplicity, suppose that there is no moderating effect. If the population correlation is zero, then there are now four opportunities to make a Type I error instead of one and the actual Type I error rate would not be .05 but .19. If the population correlation is not zero, then there are four opportunities to make a Type II error rather than just one. But the situation is worse than that. The probability of a Type I error is always .05 regardless of the sample size, but the probability of a Type II error increases drastically with a decrease in sample size. For example, if the population correlation is .20 and the sample size is 100, then the probability of statistical significance and a correct inference is only .50. But if the sample size is 25, then the probability of significance drops to .16; i.e., the investigator will be wrong 84 percent of the time. Furthermore, the probability of correctly concluding significance in all four subgroups is $(.16)^4 = .0007$, which is less than 1 in 1000. That is, analysis by subgroups for a population correlation of .20 raises the Type II error rate from 50 percent to 99.9%.

SUBGROUPS AND CAPITALIZATION ON CHANCE

The situation is even worse for the many investigators who select the data to present using significance tests. If there were 10 variables in the study, then the correlation matrix would have 45 entries. If all population correlations were 0, then the analysis of the whole sample would provide for a search through 45 entries to capitalize on chance. At least two such correlations would be expected to be significant and it would not be incredibly unlucky to get five. For a sample size of 100, the largest correlation in a chance matrix would be expected to be .23. However, for a subgroup, the largest correlation among 45 would be expected to be .46. Furthermore, the analysis by subgroups provides a search list of 4(45) = 180 elements on which to capitalize by chance, and hence a greater expected error and an expected eight and possibly twenty false significant readings.

Even if the null hypothesis were false for every correlation (in which case every failure to find significance would be a Type II error of about 84 percent frequency), the handful pulled out would be completely unrepresentative of the population correlations. The true value of each correlation is .20, but with a sample size of 25, only correlations of .40 or greater will be significant (two-tailed test, $p \leqslant .05$). Therefore, only those correlations that by chance are much larger than the population value will be statistically significant. The conclusion that these correlations are not zero will be correct; that is, in this 16 percent of cases there will be no Type II error. But these significant observed correlations will greatly overestimate actual population correlations. The significant observed correlations will in fact be about twice as large as the actual value.

SUBGROUPS AND SUPPRESSION OF DATA

There is a current practice in journals that acts to restrict publication of data. Under current pressures, it is likely that an author who analyzed four subgroups would be allowed to publish only one-fourth as much data on each group. From the point of view of future cumulation, this is a disaster. There are too many missing values as is.

SUBGROUPS AND THE BIAS OF DISAGGREGATION

If the moderator effect is nonexistent or trivial in magnitude, then the desired correlation for cumulation is the total group correlation. But for all practical purposes, it is the average correlation that is entered into the larger cumulation. That is, if there is no moderator effect, then the larger cumulation will ultimately average all entries and hence implicitly average the entries for each study. As it happens, the average correlation in this case may be quite "biased" as an estimate of the total sample correlation. This bias is always in the direction of the average correlation, being smaller in magnitude than the total sample correlation. This bias is produced by restriction in range in the subgroups.

Assume that the covariance structure is the same in each subgroup, i.e., assume that the regression line is the same in all groups. Then the correlation is smaller in a subgroup to the extent that the standard deviation in the subgroup is smaller than the total population standard deviation. Let u be the ratio of standard deviations, i.e., let u be defined by

$$u = \frac{\sigma_{subgroup}}{\sigma_{total}}$$

Let r_t be the correlation in the total group and let r_s be the correlation in the subgroup. Then the conventional formula for restriction in range yields

$$r_s = \frac{ur_t}{\sqrt{(u^2 - 1)\, r_t^2 + 1}}$$

For small correlations, this formula differs little from $r_s = ur_t$, i.e., the subgroup correlation is lower by a factor of u. To show that u is less than 1, we note that

$$u^2 = \frac{\sigma^2_{subgroup}}{\sigma^2_{total}} = 1 - \eta^2$$

where η^2 is the correlation ratio between the grouping variable and the causally prior variable of the two being correlated.

CONCLUSION: USE TOTAL GROUP CORRELATIONS

If the moderating effect of the demographic variable is to be studied, then of course subgroup correlations should be entered into the cumulation. However, once the demographic variable is known to have little or no moderating effect, then the major cumulative analysis should be done with total group correlations.

SUMMARY

There are three common forms of replication within studies: fully replicated designs, conceptual replication, and analysis of subgroups. Each requires a different strategy for meta-analysis.

A fully replicated design is a study in which there are subparts that are independent replications of the study design. For example, the same study design might be carried out in three organizations. Results from each organization can then be entered into the meta-analysis as if the results were from three separate studies. If results are averaged rather than entered separately, then the average should be treated as if the sample size were the sum of the sample sizes across the three organizations.

Conceptual replication is multiple measurement. Either the independent or the dependent variable could be measured by several instruments or methods. Each such measure could then be used to generate an alternative correlation or effect size. Ideally, these alternate measures would be combined by using confirmatory factor analysis to combine alternate measures. For example, one might sum the raw or standard scores for each alternate measure of the independent variable, and one might sum the raw or standard scores of the independent variable. These index variables would then be correlated to produce one correlation. Or the index dependent variable could be used to compute d. In either case, the study contributes one value to the meta-analysis with minimum error of measurement. If the study report does not contain the information to do a confirmatory factor analysis, then the best alternative is to average the conceptually equivalent correlations or effect sizes. Since the values are not independent, the sample size for the average is the same as the sample size for the study. The average value will be an underestimate of the value that would have been produced by confirmatory factor analysis.

Analysis of subgroups may be either important or frivolous. If the subgroups are defined by what is believed to be a large moderator variable, then there should be a corresponding meta-analysis of these subgroups across studies. However, if the analysis of subgroups simply stems from a ritual analysis by sex and race, then the total group correlation should be the only contribution to the meta-analysis. In any case, the total group correlation should be used for the main meta-analysis across studies. If the total group correlation is not given and cannot be computed from the information in the report, then the subgroup correlations should be averaged and the average correlation would be used in the meta-analysis with the total group sample size. This average correlation will usually be slightly smaller than the total group correlation.

6

Methods of Integrating
Findings Across Studies

☐ This chapter presents and critiques six different methods for integrating results across studies. These methods are presented in their approximate temporal order of development. This order is also their approximate order of efficacy (from least to most efficacious) in extracting the information needed from the studies reviewed.

THE TRADITIONAL NARRATIVE PROCEDURE

The oldest procedure, the narrative review, has also been described as "literary," "qualitative," "nonquantitative," and "verbal." In this procedure the reviewer takes each study at face value and attempts to find an overarching theory that reconciles the findings. If few studies exist, this integration can be carried out even though there may be some conflict between reviewers who postulate different interactions. But if the number of studies is large (100 to 1000), then the studies will almost never be precisely comparable in design, measures, and so forth, and findings will typically vary across studies in bizarre ways. As a result, the information-processing task becomes too taxing for the human mind. The result is usually one of three outcomes. First, the result may be "pedestrian reviewing where verbal synopses of studies are strung out in dizzying lists" (Glass, 1976, p. 4). That is, the reviewer may not even attempt to integrate findings across studies. Second, the reviewer may simplify the integration task by basing his or her conclusions on only a small subset of the studies.

Reviewers often reject all but a few of the studies as deficient in design or analysis, and then "advance the one or two acceptable studies as the truth of the matter" (Glass, 1976, p. 4). This approach unjustifiably wastes much information, and, in addition, may focus on unrepresentative studies. Third, the reviewer may actually attempt the task of mentally integrating findings across all studies—and fail to do an adequate job. Cooper and Rosenthal (1980) have shown that even when the number of studies reviewed is as small as seven, reviewers who use narrative-discursive methods and reviewers who use quantitative methods reach different conclusions.

THE TRADITIONAL VOTING METHOD

The traditional voting method was one of the first techniques developed to ease the information-processing burden on the reviewer. In its simplest form, it consists merely of a tabulation of significant and nonsignificant findings. Light and Smith (1971, p. 433) described this approach as follows:

> All studies which have data on a dependent variable and a specific independent variable of interest are examined. Three possible outcomes are defined. The relationship between the independent variable and the dependent variable is either significantly positive, significantly negative, or there is no significant relationship in either direction. The number of studies falling into each of these three categories is then simply tallied. If a plurality of studies falls into any of these three categories, with fewer falling into the other two, the model category is declared the winner. This model categorization is then assumed to give the best estimates of the direction of the true relationship between the independent and dependent variable.

The voting method is sometimes used also in an attempt to identify correlates of study outcomes. For example, the proportion of studies in which training method A was superior to training method B might be compared for males and females.

The voting method is in common use today. An example of a recent review based on this method is Eagly (1978). The voting method is biased in favor of large-sample studies that may show only small effect sizes. Even where variation in sample size does not cause problems in interpreting significance levels, and where the voting method correctly leads to the conclusion that an effect exists, the critical question of the size of the effect is still left unanswered. But the most important problem with the voting method is that it can and does lead to false conclusions. Consider an example. Based on 144 studies, Pearlman, Schmidt, and Hunter (1980) found the correlation of general intelligence and proficiency in clerical work to be .51. That is, if a perfect validity study were done using the entire applicant population and a perfectly reliable measure of job proficiency, then the correlation between intelligence and performance would be .51. But proficiency measures cannot be obtained on applicants; performance can be measured only on those who are hired. Most organizations hire fewer than half of those who apply. Suppose that those hired are those in the top half of the distribution on intelligence. Then because of restriction in range, the correlation between test and performance will only be .33 rather than .51. But it is also impossible to obtain perfect measures of job performance. Typically, the best feasible measure is the rating of the single supervisor who knows the person's work well enough to rate it. According to the review of King, Hunter, and Schmidt (1980), the usual interrater reliability of a single rating by a single supervisor is only .31. If the rater were asked to make multiple judgments and those ratings were combined into a composite score, then the correct interrater reliability would rise to .62. In this "best" of cases, the reliability of the job performance measure would be .62 (actually less, though we will ignore here the reduction in reliability produced by restriction in range) and the potential correlation between test and performance would be dropped from .33 to .26.

So because of problems inherent in doing field studies, the investigator begins work with an underlying population correlation of .26. What are the implications of doing such a study with a small sample? Suppose that Smith does a study with a sample size of thirty. Then if the expected correlation of .26 were found, it would not be statistically significant and Smith would label the test as "invalid." But suppose that Jones found the same correlation of .26 using the mean sample size reported by Lent, Aurbach, and Levin (1971), i.e., N = 68. Then the same correlation would be statistically significant and Jones would label the test as "valid." Here we have a prime example of false "conflicting results in the literature"; the same correlation can be labeled "significant" in one study but "nonsignificant" in another. Reviewers using the voting method treat all studies alike and completely ignore the fact that studies with different sample sizes have a completely different meaning for "significant."

But suppose that all studies were done with the same sample size. Would reviews find the research literature consonant with the uniformity that we have defined our example to have? Certainly not. We have assumed that the observed correlations would equal the population correlations, but this is quite false. If all studies were done with fifty subjects, what would the effect of sampling error be? For fifty subjects, the correlation must be .28 to be significant at the .05 level using a two-tailed test. Given a population correlation of .26, the observed correlation will have a mean of .26 and a standard deviation of .13. The probability that the observed correlation will be larger than .28 and hence be labeled as "significant" is .44. Thus across studies, the test would be correctly labeled "valid" 44 percent of the time and would be incorrectly labeled "invalid" 56 percent of the time. Thus the author list in the review on one side of the issue would be just about as long as the author list on the other side of the issue. Note that all authors who claim the test is "invalid" are actually wrong. That is, the conclusion stated in the *majority* of studies is wrong. Thus the "preponderance of data" using counts of statistical significance can be completely false.

Furthermore, Hedges and Olkin (1980) have pointed out (and proven) that if there is a true effect, then in any set of studies in which mean statistical power is less than about .50, the probability of a false conclusion using the voting method increases as the number of studies increases. That is, the more data examined, the greater the certainty of a false conclusion about the meaning of the data! Thus the traditional voting method is fatally flawed statistically and logically. Although reviewers using the voting method often reach conclusions—false or otherwise—the typical conclusion is that the research literature is in deplorable shape. Some researchers get results; others do not. Sometimes a given researcher gets significant results, sometimes not. These reviewers almost invariably issue pained calls for better research designs, better experimental controls, better measures, and so on (Glass, 1976).

CUMULATION OF p-VALUES ACROSS STUDIES

This procedure attempts to cumulate significance levels across studies to produce an overall p-value (significance level) for the set of studies as a whole. If this value is small enough, the reviewer concludes that the existence of the effect has been established. Methods for combining p-values across studies go back at least three decades (Baker, 1952), but the most recent advocates of this approach have been Rosenthal and his associates (Rosenthal, 1978; Cooper & Rosenthal, 1980).

The major problem with this method is that in most sets of studies the combined p-value will be significant, but that fact tells nothing about the magnitude of the effect. Obviously, the practical and theoretical implications of an effect depend at least as much on its size as on its existence. Rosenthal (1978, p. 192) has admitted the necessity for analysis of effect sizes along with p-values, and in his latest substantive review (e.g., Rosenthal & Rubin, 1978) has used a combination of p-value and effect-size analysis. Thus analysis of p-values alone now has no real advocates to our knowledge.

In passing, we note a potentially useful technique developed by Rosenthal as a result of his work in cumulating p-values across studies. This technique was developed to address the so-called "file drawer problem." Suppose a researcher has demonstrated that the combined p-value across the studies reviewed is, say, .0001, and concludes that a real effect exists. A critic could then argue that this finding is due to nonrepresentativeness of the studies reviewed, on grounds that studies not showing an effect are much less likely to have been located by the reviewer. That is, the studies with negative findings are apt to have been tucked away in file drawers rather than circulated or published. Using Rosenthal's (1979) technique, the researcher can calculate the number of missing studies showing zero effect size that would have to exist in order to bring the combined p-value down to .05, .10, or any other level. This number typically turns out to be very large, e.g., 65,000 (Rosenthal & Rubin, 1978). It is highly unlikely that there are 65,000 "lost" studies on any topic.

STATISTICALLY CORRECT
VOTE-COUNTING METHODS

Although the traditional vote-counting method is statistically and logically deficient, there are methods of cumulating research findings across studies based on vote counting that are statistically correct. These methods fall into two categories: (1) those that yield only a statistical significance level for the body of studies, and (2) those that provide a quantitative estimate of the mean effect size.

METHODS YIELDING ONLY SIGNIFICANCE LEVELS

If the null hypothesis is true, then the population correlation or effect size is in fact zero. Thus when study results are given in the form of p-values, half would be expected to be larger than .50 and half smaller than .50. The sign test can be used to test whether the observed frequencies of findings in the positive and negative directions depart significantly from the 50-50 split expected under the null hypothesis (Rosenthal, 1978; Hedges & Olkin, 1980). Alternatively, the reviewer can use a count to determine the proportion of studies reporting statistically significant findings supporting the theory (positive significant results) and test this proportion against the proportion expected under the null hypothesis (typically .05 or .01). The binomial test or the chi-square statistic can be used for this test (Brozek & Tiede, 1952; Rosenthal, 1978; Hedges & Olkin, 1980). Hedges and Olkin (1980) note that some reviewers believe that most, if not the majority, of studies should show a positive significant result if the true effect size or true correlation is nonzero. In fact, this is typically not true. When the true effect size or true correlation is in the range of magnitude typically encountered, only a minority of studies will usually report significant positive findings because of low statistical power in the individual studies. They also point out that the proportion of positive significant findings required to reject the null hypothesis is much smaller than is commonly believed. For example, if ten studies are run using alpha = .05, the probability of three or more positive significant findings is less than .01. That is, three positive significant findings out of ten is sufficient to reject the null hypothesis.

These vote-counting methods, however, are most useful when the null hypothesis is true, not when it is false. For example, Bartlett, Bobko, Mosier, and Hannon (1978) and Hunter, Schmidt, and Hunter (1979) showed that frequency of significant differences in employment test validities for blacks and whites did not differ from the chance frequencies expected under the null hypothesis and the alpha levels used. Bartlett et al., for example, examined over 1100 such tests at the alpha = .05 level and found that 6.2 percent were significant. When the null hypothesis is not rejected in cumulative studies with high statistical power, this method does provide an estimate of population effect size or population correlation: zero. However, when the null hypothesis is false, the binomial or sign tests provide no estimate of effect size. This is a serious disadvantage.

METHODS YIELDING ESTIMATES OF EFFECT SIZES

The probability of a positive result and the probability of a positive significant result are both functions of the population effect size and study sample size. If sample sizes are known for all studies, then the effect size can be estimated from either the proportion of positive results or from the proportion of positive significant results. Hedges and Olkin (1980) have derived formulas for both of these methods of estimating effect size. They also present formulas for determining the confidence intervals around the effect-size estimates. These confidence intervals will, in general, be wider than those resulting when effect sizes are determined individually for each study and then averaged, as advocated by Glass (1976). (In the latter case, confidence intervals are based on the standard error of the mean.) The confidence intervals are wider because estimation of effect sizes from counts of positive or positive significant results uses less information from the studies than the Glass (1976) procedure. Therefore, vote-counting-based estimates of effect sizes should typically only be used when the information needed to determine effect sizes in individual studies is not available or retrievable.

The Hedges and Olkin method of estimating effect size based on vote counting is based on the assumption that effect size is constant across studies. If effect sizes vary across studies, this method yields only an approximate estimate of mean effect size. Further, this method provides no estimate at all of the *variance* of effect sizes across studies.

This method of integrating findings across studies was developed only recently (Hedges & Olkin, 1980). It is therefore an exception to the rule of presenting cumulation methods in approximate temporal order of development. However, it is presented in its proper order of effectiveness or usefulness.

THE META-ANALYSIS OF
RESEARCH STUDIES

The basic concepts underlying meta-analysis were employed decades ago by Thorndike (1933) and Ghiselli (1949) and more recently by Fleishman and Levine and their associates (see Levine, Romashko, & Fleishman, 1973, Levine, Kramer, & Levine, 1975). Thorndike and Ghiselli cumulated results across studies based on the use of average correlations. Thorndike

(1933) went further and corrected the observed variance of find-ings across studies for the effects of sampling error. Fleishman and Levine and their associates cumulated effect sizes across experimental studies to determine the relation between alcohol intake and decrements in task performances dependent on differ-ent abilities (Levine, Kramer, & Levine, 1975) and to determine the effectiveness of an abilities classification system in the vigilance area of human performance (Levine, Romashko, & Fleishman, 1973). None of these authors, however, advanced a systematic body of meta-analysis methodology for use in solving the general problem of integrating findings across studies to produce cumulative knowledge. In recent years, systematic quantitative techniques for integrating research findings across studies have been introduced. Glass (1976) advanced the first such set of procedures and coined the term "meta-analysis" to refer to the analysis of analyses (studies). One reason he introduced this term was to distinguish such analyses from secondary analysis. In secondary analysis, the researcher obtains and reanalyzes the original data on which an earlier study was based (Light & Smith, 1971). In this book we use the term "meta-analysis" to refer to Glass's methods and to those we developed. Meta-analysis is the quantitative cumulation and analysis of descriptive statistics across studies. It does not require access to original study data.

GLASS'S META-ANALYSIS METHODS

The primary properties of Glass's meta-analysis are:

(1) A strong emphasis on effect sizes rather than significance levels. Glass believes the purpose of research integration is more descriptive than inferential, and he feels that the most important descriptive statistics are those that indicate most clearly the mag-nitude of effects. His meta-analysis typically employs estimates of the Pearson r or of d, where

$$d = (\bar{X}_E - \bar{X}_C)/SD$$

and $\bar{X}_E$ and $\bar{X}_C$ are the means of the experimental and control groups, respectively. SD is the average SD or the SD of the control group. Glass (1977) has presented quite a number of useful formulas for converting statistics in studies to estimates of d or r. The initial product of a Glassian meta-analysis is the mean and standard deviation of effect sizes[1] across studies (e.g., see Smith & Glass, 1977).

(2) Acceptance of the variance of effect sizes (S^2_{ES}) at face value. Glassian meta-analysis implicitly assumes that S^2_{ES} is real and should have some substantive explanation. These explanations are sought in the varying characteristics of the studies, e.g., sex or mean age of subjects, length of treatment. Study characteristics that correlate with study effect are examined for their explanatory power. The general finding has been that few study characteristics correlate significantly with study outcomes. Problems of capitalization on chance and low statistical power associated with this step in meta-analysis are discussed later in this chapter.

(3) A strongly empirical approach to determining which aspects of studies should be coded and tested for possible association with study outcomes. Glass (1976, 1977) feels that all such questions are "empirical questions," and he seems to deemphasize the role of theory or logic in determining which variables should be tested as potential moderators of study outcome (see also, Glass, 1972).

Glassian meta-analysis has been applied to research studies on the effects of psychotherapy (Smith & Glass, 1977), the effects of the Keller personalized instruction system (Kulik, Kulik, & Cohen, 1979), gender effects in sensitivity to nonverbal cues (Hall, 1978), and to other sets of research studies. In each case, the results clarify what was previously a confusing set of results and allow fairly specific conclusions.

THE SCHMIDT-HUNTER META-ANALYSIS METHODS: VALIDITY GENERALIZATION

This procedure was developed concurrently with Glass's work for application to validity studies of employment tests (Schmidt & Hunter, 1977; Schmidt, Hunter, Pearlman & Shane, 1979; Pearlman, Schmidt, & Hunter, 1980; Schmidt, Gast-Rosenberg,

& Hunter, 1980); however, its principles are general and have been extended to other research areas (Hunter, 1979). Even though its developers were unaware of Glass's work at the time, this procedure can be regarded as an extension of Glassian meta-analysis to deal with problems such as sampling error, unreliability, restriction in range, and the like. The primary properties of this procedure are:

(1) A strong emphasis on effect sizes rather than p-values. This emphasis is pretty much the same as that in Glassian meta-analysis, and for the same reasons. Effect sizes are expressed as correlations, but this is not an important distinction. Unlike Glassian meta-analysis, this meta-analysis procedure calls for correcting the mean effect size for attenuation due to instrument unreliability and range restriction (if any), yielding more accurate estimates of mean effect sizes.

(2) Unlike Glassian meta-analysis, Schmidt-Hunter meta-analysis does not take S^2_{ES} at face value. Instead, the first order of business after determination of the mean effect size is to test the hypothesis that S^2_{ES} is entirely due to various statistical artifacts. These artifacts include: (a) sampling error, (b) study differences in reliability of independent and dependent variable measures, (c) study differences in range restriction, (d) study differences in instrument validity, and (e) computational, typographical, and transcription errors. Schmidt and Hunter have developed methods of estimating and subtracting variance due to the first three of these five artifacts. Generally, if these three artifacts account for 75 percent or more of the observed S^2_{ES}, they conclude that the residual S^2_{ES} is probably due to the remaining two artifacts and that true $S^2_{ES} = 0$. Over a series of 152 such applications, the average amount of observed S^2_{ES} accounted for my statistical artifacts a, b, and c above has been 72 percent.

(3) If the hypothesis $S^2_{ES} > 0$ is not rejected, S^2_{ES} adjusted for the effects of the three artifacts (S^2_{ES}) is used (with the appropriate correction) to place a confidence or credibility interval around the estimated true mean effect size. (Generally, only the lower bound of this interval is emphasized in practical applications involving employment testing; see Schmidt, Gast-Rosenberg, & Hunter, 1980 for complete details).

STATE-OF-THE-ART META-ANALYSIS

As Hunter (1979) pointed out, there is no incompatibility between the Glass meta-analysis methods and the Schmidt-Hunter meta-analysis methods. The Schmidt-Hunter procedures are merely an extension of Glassian meta-analysis to deal with variations in study effect sizes due to sampling error and other artifacts and with attenuation of effect-size estimates due to measurement unreliability and range restriction. Both of these meta-analysis methods, however, are incomplete. Hunter (1979) has rewritten the Schmidt-Hunter formulas to be appropriate for use with experimental studies (where d rather than r is the effect-size statistic). These formulas are given in Chapter 4. These extensions, when combined with a provision for regressing study effect sizes on study characteristics when observed S^2_{ES} is not due completely to artifacts, yield what we refer to as "state-of-the-art meta-analysis"—that is, the most complete meta-analysis procedure now known.

The primary properties of this meta-analysis procedure are as follows:

(1) Primary focus is on effect sizes. All effect sizes are to be corrected for statistical and measurement artifacts (e.g., instrument unreliability) that attenuates them from their true score values.

(2) After estimating mean true effect size, the hypothesis that observed S^2_{ES} is due to statistical artifacts is tested, using methods developed by Schmidt and Hunter. This is the hypothesis that $S^2_{ESA} > 0$. If this hypothesis is rejected, the reviewer concludes that ES is constant across the many factors varying in the studies reviewed. Estimated $\overline{ESA}$ is then the final and only product of the review.

(3) If the hypothesis that $S^2_{ESA} > 0$ cannot be rejected, then selected properties that vary across studies are coded and correlated with study ESs as suggested by Glass—except that one relies upon theoretical, logical, statistical, and psychometric considerations when possible in deciding what study characteristics to code and how to code them. Study properties coded should not be the artifacts (or products of the artifacts) controlled for in step 2; otherwise, the effects of a given artifact may be partialed out twice.

(4) Correlations between study characteristics and ESs are corrected for sampling error in ESs using the procedure developed by Hunter (1979). (This procedure can be expanded to include correction for unreliability in the study characteristic if it is not perfectly assessed.) If all these correlations are trivial in magnitude, go to step 8.

(5) Correlations among study characteristics are computed and corrected for unreliability in the study characteristics.

(6) The true score regression of ES on study characteristics is computed. The resulting beta weights should be interpreted as indicating potential causal effects of true study characteristics on true study ESs.

(7) The resulting true score multiple R should be corrected for shrinkage using the appropriate shrinkage formula (Cattin, 1980). This shrunken R^2 then gives the percentage variance in S^2_{ESA} (from step 2) accounted for by variation in study characteristics. (Unfortunately, however, this procedure will often not fully correct for capitalization on chance. See the discussion of capitalization on chance below.)

(8) Three different kinds of distributions of ES can then be derived. These constitute the final products of the meta-analysis:

(a) $\overline{X} = \overline{ESA}$, with standard deviation corrected for effects of statistical artifacts only. This distribution describes true effect sizes to be expected when study characteristics are allowed to vary as in reviewed studies. This would be the information needed if, for example, a given educational program were to be implemented in somewhat different ways in different parts of the country. Confidence intervals are derived for this distribution.

(b) $\overline{X} = \overline{ESA}$ with standard deviation corrected for effects of statistical artifacts *and for effects of deviations of study characteristics from their mean values.* This distribution describes true ES to be expected when study characteristics are held constant at their mean values. Confidence intervals can be derived for this distribution.

(c) The value of $\overline{X} = \overline{ESA}$ and the standard deviation can be found for a distribution in which study characteristics are held constant at values other than their means. Under the usual assumption of homoscedasticity, all such alternative sets of study characteristic values should leave SD_{ESA} unchanged from distribution b. However, $\overline{ESA}$ would change. Thus a decision maker could specify in advance the conditions of implementation and compute the expected ES under that specific set of conditions. He or she could then construct a confidence interval for the ES. This ability to tailor effect size predictions to specific sets of circumstances could be useful to decision makers.

In cases in which study characteristics do not correlate with ES, the distributions in a, b, and c will be identical. In such a case, the combination procedure reduces to the Schmidt-Hunter procedure. The combination procedure also reduces to the Schmidt-Hunter procedure for data sets in which it is concluded that artifacts fully account for observed S^2_{ES}.

In both Glass's meta-analysis and in the state-of-the-art meta-analysis, there is an unsolved problem. When effect size estimates are regressed on multiple study characteristics, capitalization on chance operates to increase the apparent number of significant associations. Since the sample size is the *number of studies* and many study properties may be coded, this problem is potentially severe. There is no purely statistical solution to this problem. The problem can be mitigated, however, by basing choice of study characteristics and final conclusions not only on the statistics at hand, but also on other theoretically relevant findings (which may be the results of other meta-analyses) and on theoretical considerations. Results should be examined closely for substantive and theoretical meaning. Capitalization on chance is a threat whenever the (unknown) correlation or regression weight is actually zero or near zero. When there is in fact a substantial relationship, there is another problem: Statistical power to detect the relation may be low. Thus true moderators of study outcomes (to the extent that such exist) may have only a low probability of showing up as statistically significant. In short, this step in meta-analysis is often plagued with all the problems of small-sample studies. For a discussion of these problems, see Schmidt, Hunter, and Urry (1976) and Schmidt and Hunter (1978).

SUMMARY OF REVIEW

We have reviewed eight different methods for integrating research findings across studies. These methods form a rough continuum of efficacy in revealing hidden facts that can be proven by the cumulative weight of previous studies. The narrative method is unsystematic, haphazard, and imposes an impossible information-processing burden on the reviewer. The traditional voting method uses only part of the available information, provides no information about effect size, and—worst of all—logically leads to false conclusions under circumstances that are quite common. Cumulating p-values across studies does not logically lead to false conclusions, but has all the other disadvantages of the traditional voting method. Statistically correct vote-counting methods that yield only an overall statistical significance level (p-value) for the group of studies reviewed here have all the disadvantages of cumulating p-values across studies. In particular, these methods provide no estimate of effect size. Other vote-counting procedures presented by Hedges and Olkin (1980) do provide estimates of effect size, but the uncertainty in such estimates is substantial because these methods are based on only a part of the information in the individual studies. These methods also require the assumption that effect sizes are equal across studies; if this assumption is not met, then these methods yield only an approximate estimate of *mean* effect size. Also, if this assumption is not met one then needs an estimate of the *variance* of effect sizes across studies, and these methods provide no estimate of this variance.

Glassian meta-analysis is a quantum improvement over these research integration methods. It uses more of the available information from individual studies and provides a more accurate estimate of effect size or mean effect size, it does not require the assumption that effect sizes are constant across studies, and it provides an estimate of the variance of effect sizes. It also provides for correlating study effect sizes with study characteristics in an attempt to determine the causes of variation in study findings.

The Schmidt-Hunter meta-analysis procedure used in validity generalization studies also does not require the assumption of constant effect sizes across studies. This method extends and improves Glass's methods by (1) introducing a more accurate estimate of effect size (sample-size-weighted estimates), (2) correcting effect-size estimates to remove the artifactual attenuating effects of instrument unreliability and range restriction, and (3) providing tests of the hypothesis that the variance in observed effect sizes (S^2_{ES}) is due solely to artifacts. However, it does not include the step of correlating study characteristics with study effect sizes when S^2_{ES} cannot be accounted for solely by artifacts.

The final form of meta-analysis, the Hunter-Schmidt procedure, calls for examination of these relationships when appropriate. This method also extends the earlier Schmidt-Hunter method by providing formulas for using the method with d statistics as well as with r statistics. The last procedure we refer to as state-of-the-art meta-analysis. Even this procedure, however, does not solve all problems. If effect sizes are regressed on study characteristics—which is often not necessary—there may be substantial problems of capitalization on chance and low statistical power.

CRITIQUE OF CONTEMPORARY
REVIEW PRACTICES

It would be instructive to know where contemporary reviews tend to fall along the continuum formed by these methods. To our knowledge, only one study has been done examining and evaluating published reviews.

Jackson (1978) randomly sampled 36 review articles from leading journals in education, psychology, and sociology. He found that only three (8.3 percent) of these reviews cited the mean, range, or other summary indicator of the findings of the studies reviewed. (This count includes summary indicators that focus on p-values as well as on effect sizes.) Fully eighteen of these reviews (50%) indulged in the practice of citing only the studies that supported some proposition while ignoring other studies. Half the studies failed to record the magnitude or direction of effect sizes, focusing solely on significance levels. Five reviews (14 percent) used statistical significance counting methods similar to the voting method. Only two reviews used univariate statistics to relate study characteristics to study outcomes. None used multivariate statistics for this purpose, but twelve reviews discursively discussed the possible relation of at least one study characteristic to study outcomes.

To the extent that this sample of 36 reviews is representative, these findings indicate that most reviews in psychology, education, and sociology are conducted using traditional narrative discursive methods, with a minority being based on some version of the voting method. If this is indeed the case, it is understandable that the typical reviewer erroneously concludes that the research literature is in horrible shape.

NOTE

1. In purely correlational studies, the r statistic should not, strictly speaking, be referred to as an estimate of "effect size." However, for the sake of brevity and convenience, the term "effect size" is used here to refer to both r and d. This convention is widely used.

7

The Literature Search
What Should Be Published and How To Find It

CONDUCTING A THOROUGH
LITERATURE SEARCH

There are three major approaches to locating research studies on a given topic: examining indexes to documents, searching existing bibliographies, and querying other scholars who might be familiar with appropriate studies. During the last fifteen years there have been tremendous changes in the nature of indexes to documents. For example, the SOCIAL SCISEARCH system now permits a forward citation search, i.e., a search for the studies published *after* a key article that cite that key article. Most of the following discussion will focus on the use of these indexes, but the use of bibliographies and personal queries will be briefly touched upon.

INDEXES

Existing indexes vary along several different dimensions. These include the following:

(1) *Subjects covered.* Different indexes cover different subjects, but there is a moderate degree of overlap among some indexes to the social sciences. Ten indexes that might be useful for identifying research of interest to organizational psychologists will be briefly described below.

(2) *Thoroughness of coverage.* This depends primarily on: (a) the types of documents that are indexed (which could include books,

monographs, journal articles, papers presented at regular professional meetings, reports of federally supported research, summaries of work in progress, and/or other "fugitive literature"); (b) the number of sources of each type of document that are indexed (such as 200 journals versus 500); (c) the starting date of coverage; and (d) whether or not all articles or reports from a given source (such as a specific journal or professional meeting) are indexed.

(3) *Form of the index.* Some indexes are only in printed form, some are only in machine-readable form, and some are in both printed and machine-readable form.

(4) *The kinds of information provided in the index.* Some indexes only provide the full source citation, but some provide the source citation, subject descriptors, a substantial abstract, and other information.

(5) *Availability.* Indexes in printed form are available primarily in libraries or from the publisher. Indexes in machine-readable form may be purchased or leased. More commonly they are searched by on-line access to the data files of several information retrieval systems. The most widely used are those of Bibliographic Retrieval Services, Inc., Lockheed Information Systems (Dialog), and Systems Development Corporation (Orbit).

Because of the variations in different indexes, the use of two or more of them will usually result in a larger number of appropriate citations than would the search of just one. The characteristics of ten indexes that might be of use to organizational psychologists are shown in Table 7.1.

Organizational psychologists will usually identify a larger number of appropriate studies when using *Psychological Abstracts (PA)* than when using any other one index. But the Smithsonian Science Education Exchange (SSIE) covers studies that are hardly ever in *PA* at the time of a given search. The National Technical Information Service (NTIS) covers a substantial number of studies not in *PA*. CURRENT CONTENTS lists many articles one to five months prior to their citation in most other indexes. SOCIAL SCISEARCH allows a forward citation search, which is impossible with any of the other listed indexes. And the five other indexes listed in the table will often

TABLE 7.1

Index Name	Subject Coverage	Types of Documents	Approximate Number of Publications Covered	Starting Date (printed/machine-readable form)
ABI/INFORM	All aspects of management and administration.	Journals, business magazines, and newspapers.	400	X/1971
ERIC (Education Resources Information Center)	Education and topics relevant to it such as personnel services, education management, and tests and measurement.	Journals, most government-sponsored research on education, papers presented at meetings, and other fugitive materials.	700	1966/1966
Comprehensive Dissertation Abstracts	All subjects.	Doctoral dissertations, listed University Microfilms publications of Dissertation Abstract International, American Doctors Dissertations, and Comprehensive Dissertation Index.	–	1861/1861
Management (Management Contents)	All aspects of business and management.	U.S. and non-U.S. journals, proceedings and transactions related to business and management.	–	X/1974
NTIS (National Technical Information Service)	Physical, social engineering life sciences, including administration, behavior and society, business and economics, and communication.	Government-sponsored research, journal articles, and translations prepared by or for the federal government.	–	1964/1964
Psychological Abstracts	Psychology and topics relevant to it.	Journals, technical reports and monographs books, Dissertation Abstracts International.	900	1927/1967
SOCIAL SCISEARCH (Social Science Citation Index)	Social, behavioral, and related sciences.	Journals in the social, natural, physical, and biomedical sciences.	3800	1972/1972
SSIE (Smithsonian Science Information Exchange)	Physical, social, engineering and life sciences, including behavioral sciences and social sciences.	Project descriptions from 1300 organizations that fund research (see comments).	–	X/last 24 months
Sociological Abstracts	Sociology and topics relevant to it including social psychology, management, and complex organizations.	Journals, other serials, monographs, and papers presented at meetings.	1200	X/1963

TABLE 7.1 (Continued)

Approximate Number of New Citations Each Year	Kinds of Information in the Record[a]	Approximate On-Line Connect Charge, Assuming Moderate Quantity Discount	Availability	Comments
17,000	Title, authors, source, and abstract.	$55/hr	BRS Lockheed	
36,000	Title, authors, source, descriptors, identifiers, abstract, and other.	$20/hr	BRS Lockheed SDC	
42,000	Title author, date, university, and reference if it is abstracted in Dissertation Abstracts International on American Doctoral Dissertations.	$40/hr	BRS Lockheed SDC	Has about 99% of American doctoral dissertations, and thousands of Canadian and other foreign ones.
12,000		$55/hr	BRS Lockheed SDC	
60,000	Title, author, source, descriptors, identifiers, abstract, and other.	$30/hr	BRS Lockheed SDC	Has reports to or by 300 government agencies, but thoroughness of coverage varies among agencies and over years. Coverage of behavioral and social science research is poor for the years prior to the mid-1970s.
30,000	Title, author, source, descriptors, identifiers, abstracts, and other.	$50/hr	APA, BRS Lockheed SDC	
108,000	Title, author, source, cited references, and other.	$55/hr	BRS Lockheed SDC	For each indexed article, the author and source (but not title) of each reference is given. In addition, for each author there is a list of any of his or her articles which have been referenced in other indexed articles, with the names of the author(s) who referred to each particular article.
108,000	Title, author, source, descriptors, abstract, and other.	$65/hr	BRS Lockheed SDC	Has descriptions of research that is in process or recently completed. Includes most federal government contract and grant research; other covered funding resources include state and local governments, foundations, universities, and so on.
7500	Title, author, source, descriptors, identifiers, abstract, and other.	$40/hr	Lockheed	

a. Descriptors are subject terms specified in a thesaurus; identifiers are subject terms usually chosen at the discretion of the indexer.

identify at least a few appropriate studies not found through the use of *Psychological Abstracts.*

When an index is available in both printed and machine-readable form, there are several points worth remembering when deciding which to use.

(1) The biggest advantages of computerized searches of machine-readable files are speed and accuracy.

(2) Usually both forms of the index will cover the same documents and have the same kinds of information about the documents.

(3) The machine-readable forms seldom cover documents released prior to the mid-1960s. Because of this, but usually only because of it, the coverage of the machine-readable form is often less thorough than that of the printed form.

(4) Some machine-readable index files are considerably cheaper to search than others. Generally the government supported or maintained files are the cheapest, running $25-$40 per connect hour, and the proprietary files are the most expensive, running $60-$80 per hour.

(5) It will take about two days to become fairly competent using any of the major computerized information retrieval systems that access the indexes, and another day or two to acquire a good knowledge of each index you wish to search. Consequently, if you do searches infrequently, it may pay to have an experienced information specialist do them. You might find one at your university library or computer center. Most of the organizations (including the American Psychological Association) that produce the indexes will conduct, on a fee-for-services basis, a search of their own index.

BIBLIOGRAPHIES AND PERSONAL QUERIES

Searching bibliographies of previous reviews and documents on the topic is a time-honored approach for locating appropriate studies.

Querying scholars who might be familiar with appropriate studies is also a widely used approach. We suspect it is most effective when you include with your letter a copy of the bibliography that you have compiled to that date, and a self-addressed stamped envelope. A query of "Please inform me of all studies on topic X that you are aware of" usually requires substantially more effort to answer than listing a few studies that one notices are not on the enclosed bibliography.

When a research topic is fairly new, this often is the most productive search approach. It was by far the most productive approach when we did our search for the preparation of this book.

WHAT TO DO ABOUT STUDIES WITH "METHODOLOGICAL WEAKNESSES"

Many reviewers wish to eliminate from their analyses studies that they perceive as having methodological inadequacies. This often is not as reasonable and desirable as it may seem. The assertion of "methodological inadequacy" always depends on theoretical assumptions about what *might* be true in a study. These assumptions may well be false and are rarely tested in their own right. Those who believe the assumptions feel no need to test them. That is, the hypothesis of "methodological inadequacy" is rarely tested empirically. No research study can be defended against all possible counterhypotheses; hence no study can be "without methodological inadequacy." However, methodological inadequacies do not always cause biased findings; and prior to the analyses of the full set of studies on the topic it is difficult to determine reliably when methodological inadequacies have caused biased findings and when they have not.

Some reviewers are inclined to use the simple strategy of eliminating all the studies with methodological inadequacies. Since most studies have some weaknesses, these reviewers often end up reporting inferences based on only a few studies. When there is good a priori evidence that the eliminated studies had substantially biased results this strategy would be justified, but that seldom is the case.

The hypothesis of methodological inadequacy should be tested only after two prior hypotheses have been rejected: First, one should determine if the variation across all studies can be accounted for by sampling error and other artifacts such as differences in reliability. If the variation is due solely to artifacts, then there can be no variance due to methodological inadequacy. Second, if there is substantial variation across studies, then theoretically plausible moderator variables should be tested. If the moderator variables account for all nonartifactual variance, then there can be no variance due to methodological inadequacy. If the theoretically plausible moderator variables do not explain the variance, then methodological inadequacies may be present. One can then rate the internal and external validity of the studies or code the characteristics that might produce inadequacy and test these characteristics as moderator variables.

Several readers have suggested that there is a counterexample to our argument: violations of construct validity across studies. Just because the same variable name is used in different studies does not mean that the same variable is measured in those studies. We believe that construct validity is an empirical rather than theoretical question. Ideally, one would do an empirical study in which all alternative instruments or methods are used to measure the independent and dependent variables. Confirmatory factor analysis could then be used to see if the alternate measures differ by more than random error of measurement. A much inferior test of the construct invalidity hypothesis can be run within a meta-analysis. If several instruments are really measuring different things, then it seems unlikely that they would have the same correlation with the second variable of the meta-analysis (or that the treatment effect would be identical across the different variables). If the meta-analysis shows no variance across studies, then that would suggest that the alternate measures are substantially equivalent. On the other hand, if the meta-analysis does find variance across studies, then the hypothesized nonequivalence of variables can be used as a moderator variable. If this does explain the variance across studies, then there is confirmation of the hypothesis of construct invalidity. In any case, it is our belief that the *assertion* of construct invalidity is not the same as the *fact* of construct invalidity. We believe that methodological hypotheses are less likely to be true than substantive hypotheses since they are usually based on fewer data.

It is important to recognize that the actual threat to the internal and external validity of a study is not determined exclusively or even primarily by the design of the study. Campbell and Stanley's monograph (1963) on experimental and quasi-experimental design shows which threats are controlled by various different designs if none of the controlled factors interact. But the mono-graph does not indicate which threats are likely to be trivial in a given study or which threats can be reasonably controlled by other means.

REPORTING A REVIEW

A widely held precept in all the sciences is that reports of research ought to include enough information about the study so that the reader can critically examine the evidence. As a minimum, it is held that the report ought to describe the sampling, measure-ment, analyses, and the findings. Where unusual procedures have been used, it is expected that they will be described in some detail.

Researchers are never more acutely aware of the importance of these reporting standards than when they are reviewing a set of studies. Inadequate reports of primary research add tremendously to the burden of doing any kind of review. But, ironically, reports of reviews probably violate these precepts more often than do reports of primary research. Jackson's (1978) analysis of 36 review articles in quality journals found that only four reported major aspects of the search for relevant studies; only seven indicated whether or not the full set of located studies on the topic was analyzed; just half of the 36 reported the direction and magni-tude of the findings of *any* of the primary studies; and only three cited the mean, range, or another summary of the magnitude of the primary study's findings.

The consequences of such reporting omissions are serious. There are two reasons for carefully describing the literature search process in a review article. First, it helps the reader to judge the comprehensiveness and representativeness of the sources that are the subject of the review. Second, briefly detailing the litera-ture search process in a review article allows future reviewers of the topic to extend the review without duplicating it. If it is known that most of the articles included in the review were those listed under certain descriptors of certain years of certain indexes, or found in the bibliographies of specified sources, it is very easy for a subsequent reviewer to broaden or deepen the search for rele-vant sources without duplicating the earlier work.

Excluding some located studies on a given topic from the analysis of a review can seriously affect the inferences drawn from the review. Readers need to know whether or not there may be such an effect. And if some studies are excluded, the criteria for exclusion, the number of studies excluded, and the citations of the excluded studies are useful to the critical reader.

The direction and magnitude of each primary study finding or of the mean or variance of the set of findings is important information. Without it the reader often cannot make even a preliminary judgment about the validity of a review's conclusions unless he or she laboriously consults the original reports of each study. Many reviews do not cover more than forty or fifty studies. In such cases it is often possible to provide substantial data on each study in a single-page table. The table should include the author and date of each study, the sample size, and the standardized effect score. If sources of spurious variance do not account for most of the variation in the standardized effect scores, other characteristics of each study should be included, such as the status characteristics of the subjects, subjects' average pretreatment scores on the criterion (when applicable), level and duration or scope conditions (such as region of the country, occupations of subjects, and the like), strength of the study design with respect to internal and external validity, and other study characteristics. If there is not enough space for this table in the publication, there should be a reference indicating where it can be obtained.

INFORMATION NEEDED IN
REPORTS OF PRIMARY RESEARCH

The Hunter/Schmidt/Glass meta-analysis procedure needs certain kinds of data from each primary study that are to be included in the cumulation. Unfortunately, some of those data are usually missing from at least a few of the studies being reviewed. This forces the reviewer to track down authors and try to secure the data from them, and when that fails, to "guesstimate" it. Often the missing data would lengthen the report of the study by only one-fourth to one-half of a page, and in all cases this data would provide the readers important information about the study as well as provide a basis for valid accumulations. Large correlation matrices may be awkward to include in some reports, but this primary data should be preserved for later analysis and referenced in the report.

CORRELATIONAL STUDIES

Consider first correlational studies. If reported study findings are to be usable in cumulative studies, then the mean, standard deviation, and reliability of each variable should be published. The mean is necessary for the cumulation of norms, for the cumulation of regression lines (or for the assessment of possible non-linearity over extreme ranges), or for the identification of very special populations. The standard deviation is necessary for the same reasons and for a further one. If the relation between two variables is linear, then there is little variation in the correlation produced by variation in the mean from study to study. However, this is quite different for the standard deviation. Differences in variability from study to study can have dramatic effects on variable intercorrelations. If a study is being done in a homogeneous population in which the standard deviation is only half the size of the standard deviation in other studies, then in that population the correlations for that variable would be only about half the size of correlations observed in the other populations. Similarly, if the variance is inflated by observing only high and low extreme groups on a given variable, then correlations for that study would be higher than in a population with the middle range included. The reliability is needed for two reasons. First, variations in standard deviation produce differences in the reliability. Second, and more importantly, the variable used in the study may not be identical to that used in published norm studies. For example, a study might include a measure of "authoritarianism," but that scale might consist of a subset of eight items chosen by the investigator; the reliability of this subscale may be quite different from the reliability for the whole scale published in norm studies. In the case of new scales, reliabilities may not have been established on large norm populations; in such cases the reliabilities can be established by cumulating across studies.

It is imperative that the entire matrix of zero-order correlations between all variables be published (note that the means, standard deviations, and reliabilities can be easily appended as extra rows or columns of this matrix). Each entry in this table may be used in entirely unrelated cumulation studies. Correlations that are not statistically significant should still be included; one cannot average a "—" or an "ns" or a "..." or whatever. If only significant correlations were printed, then cumulation would necessarily be biased. This is even more the case for correlations that are not even mentioned because they are not significant.

Moreover, there is a prevalent misperception concerning "nonsignificant" correlations. Many believe that nonsignificant means that no statistically significant finding could be associated with those variables in that study. This is not in fact the case. The size of a correlation is relative to the context in which it is considered; partial correlations and beta weights may be much larger than zero-order correlations. For example, suppose that we find a nonsignificant correlation of .10 between performance of supervisor and subordinate performance. If composite ability of subordinates were correlated .70 with their performance but not with quality of supervision, then the partial correlation between quality of supervision and subordinate performance with subordinate ability held constant would rise to .14, which might then be statistically significant. If motivation of subordinates were correlated .70 with their performances but were uncorrelated with their abilities, then the double partial correlation of quality of supervision and subordinate performance with both ability and motivation controlled would be .71, which would be highly significant. Thus although quality of supervision might not be significantly correlated with subordinate performance at a zero level, it might be highly correlated when extraneous variables are controlled. To say the same thing another way, even though an independent variable is not significantly correlated with a dependent variable, its beta weight in a multiple regression might be highly statistically significant. This is another important reason why all zero-order correlations should be included in published studies.

EXPERIMENTAL STUDIES

What about experimental studies in which analysis of variance is used instead of correlation? In a two-group design, the F value that is conventionally computed is an exact transformation of the point-biserial correlation. The significance test on the point-biserial correlation is exactly equivalent to the F test. In a 2 by 2 by 2 by . . . design, every effect in the analysis of variance is the comparison of two means and could thus be represented by a point-biserial correlation. In fact, the square of that point-biserial correlation is the "eta square" or percentage of variance accounted for by that effect. In designs with more than two categories for a facet, the categories are frequently ordered (indeed frequently quantitative). In such cases, there is rarely any significant effect beyond the linear trend. In any case, the eta squared (or better, the appropriate square root) can be used as a correlation between the corresponding variables. Thus everything stated above, including considerations of restrictions in range and reliability, is just as true of experimental as of correlational studies.

STUDIES USING MULTIPLE REGRESSION

A multiple regression analysis of a primary study is based on the full zero-order correlation matrix for the set of predictor variables and the criterion variable. Similarly, a cumulation of multiple regression analyses must be based on a cumulative zero-order correlation matrix. But many reports of multiple regression fail to report the full correlation matrix, usually omitting the zero-order correlations among the predictors and sometimes even the zero-order correlations between each predictor and the criterion. Reporting practices may have become even worse recently. Some studies now report only the multiple regression weights for the predictors. But cumulation leading to optimal estimates of multiple regression weights requires cumulation of the predictor intercorrelations as well as of the predictor-dependent variable correlations. That is, the formula for each multiple regression weight uses all the correlations between the predictors, and hence they must be cumulatively estimated.

The practice of ignoring the predictor intercorrelations is extremely frustrating even if large samples are used. Given the predictor intercorrelations, path analysis can be used to test hypotheses about direct and indirect causes. If the predictor intercorrelations are not given, one cannot distinguish between a predictor that makes no contribution and a predictor that makes a strong but indirect contribution. In short, one cannot do the desired path analysis unless the predictor correlations are given as well as the predictor criterion correlations.

Finally, it should be noted that regression weights are not suitable for cumulation. Suppose that Y is to be predicted from X_1, X_2, . . . X_m. The beta weight for X_1 depends not only on the variables X_1 and Y, but on all the other variables, X_2, X_3, . . . contained in the same regression equation. That is, beta weights are relative to the set of predictors considered and will only replicate across studies if the exact set of predictors is considered in each. If any predictor is added or subtracted from one study to the next, then the beta weights for all variables may change. While it may be worthwhile to calculate beta weights within a study, it is crucial for cumulation purposes that the zero-order correlations be included in the published study. *After* cumulation of zero-order correlations, a multiple regression can be run using a set of predictors that may never have occurred together in any one study.

For example, suppose that we wanted to predict job performance from three abilities a, b, and c. In order to cumulate beta weights, we would have to find either (1) studies that computed beta weights for the a, b, and c combination, or (2) studies that contained a, b, and c as a subset and that published the full set of predictor intercorrelations. On the other hand, cumulation from zero-order correlations greatly expands the set of studies that can contribute estimates of one or more of the needed correlations. In fact any predictive study using a or b or c would contain at least one correlation of interest. In order for r_{ab} to be estimated, there must be at least one study with both a and b; estimation of r_{ac} requires at least one study with both a and c; and estimation of r_{bc} requires at least one study with both b and c. However, there need be no study in which all three predictors occurred together.

STUDIES USING FACTOR ANALYSIS

Factor analyses are often published and the zero-order correlation matrix omitted, presumably to conserve journal space. But zero-order correlations can be cumulated across studies while factor loadings cannot be cumulated. First, the factors that appear in a given study are not determined by the single variables that appear, but by the sets or clusters of variables that occur. For example, suppose a study contains one good measure of motivation and ten cognitive ability measures. Then it is likely that the communality of the motivation variable will be zero, and motivation will not appear in the factor analysis. Factors are defined by *redundant* measurement; no factor will appear unless it is measured by at least two redundant indicators (and preferably by three). Second, the factors in an exploratory factor analysis (such as principal axis factors followed by VARIMAX rotation) are not defined independently of one another. For example, suppose that in the initial output one cluster of variables defines G_1 and another cluster defines G_2 and the correlation between G_1 and G_2 is r. Then if factor scores are standardized the VARIMAX factors will be defined by

$$F_1 = G_1 - \alpha G_2$$

$$F_2 = G_2 - \alpha G_1$$

where

$$\alpha = \frac{1 - \sqrt{1 - r^2}}{r}$$

Thus each orthogonal factor is defined as a discrepancy variable between natural clusters. Thus the loading of an indicator of G_1 on factor F_1 will depend not only on the other indicators of G_1 in its own set but also on what other factors appear in the same study. Cluster analysis results and confirmatory factor analysis results present a somewhat different picture. If a cluster analysis or confirmatory factor analysis model fits the data (Hunter, 1980; Hunter & Gerbing, 1982, Note 3), then the factor loading of an indicator onto its own factor is the square root of its reliability and is independent of the rest of the variables and is thus subject to cumulation. However, high-quality confirmatory factor analyses are still quite rare in the literature.

STUDIES USING CANONICAL CORRELATION

Canonical correlation begins with a set of predictor variables and a set of dependent measures, and is thus conceptually a situation suitable for multiple regression. But in canonical correlation, two *new* variables are formed: a weighted combination of the predictor variables and a weighted combination of the dependent measures. These combinations are formed in such a way as to maximize the correlation between them.

Canonical correlations are not subject to cumulation across studies. Neither are the canonical weights. In multiple regression, each beta weight depends on the dependent variable and on the specific set of predictors. Thus it generalizes only to other studies in which exactly the same set of predictors is used (which is rare indeed). But each canonical regression weight depends not only on the exact set of predictors in the study, but on the exact set of dependent measures as well. Thus it will be very rare that the results of canonical regression can be compared or cumulated. On the other hand, the zero-order correlation matrices of such studies can be cumulated across studies.

STUDIES USING MULTIVARIATE ANALYSIS OF VARIANCE (MANOVA)

Statistically, MANOVA is a canonical regression, with the treatment contrast variables as "independent" variables and with the measured variables as "dependent" measures. Consequently, the data needed for cumulation across studies are the set of zero-order correlations between contrasts, between contrasts and other measured variables, and between other measured variables.

GENERAL COMMENTS

For multiple regression, factor analysis, and canonical correlation analyses, the zero-order correlation matrices are essential for cumulations across studies. And once these data are secured, the reviewer is able to analyze the cumulative correlation matrix using any appropriate statistical procedure. For example, data gathered for multiple regression can be used for path analysis.

If journals required the publication of confidence intervals in place of, or in addition to, levels of statistical significance, three benefits would ensue. First, researchers would be alerted to how much uncertainty there is in estimates derived from most individual social science studies. The common small-sample studies will generally have wide confidence intervals. Second, the results across studies would correctly appear more uniform than they usually do when focusing on the proportion of studies that are statistically significant. For instance, if there are five studies, each with a sample size of fifty, and with correlations of –.05, .13, .24, .33, and .34, only two of the five are statistically significant at the .05 level, but the .05 level confidence intervals (+ .286) of all five correlations would overlap substantially. And third, in the case of two sample t tests, reports of the CI and sample sizes are all that is needed for computing standardized effect scores.

When measures of variables with less than perfect reliability are used, should the correlations between such measures be corrected for attenuation due to error of measurement? It is clear from measurement theory that the reduction of correlations due to the use of imperfect measurement is purely a matter of artifact. Reliability of measurement is a matter of feasibility and practicality independent of the theoretical and psychological meaning of the variables measured. Thus it is correlations between perfectly measured variables that are of theoretical importance; i.e., it is the corrected correlations that should be used in analysis of variance, multiple correlation, or path analysis. If the reliability of each variable is published, those cumulating findings across studies can analyze the data using appropriate methods. Cumulation should ideally be done on corrected correlations (though as shown in the work of Schmidt and Hunter and associates, this correction can sometimes be made after the cumulation). As noted earlier, correction increases the sampling error in the estimated correlation, and therefore the formulas for the correction of variance due to sampling error in uncorrected correlation coefficients are not appropriate for correlations corrected for attenuation. Instead, the modified formulas given earlier in this book should be used to compute the sampling error in corrected correlations.

8

Summary

☐ The goal of research in any area is the production of an integrated statement of the findings of the many pieces of research done in that area. In a broad sense, this means a theoretical analysis of how the many facts fit together. However, this broad theoretical integration cannot be put on a sound footing until a narrower integration of the literature has taken place. We must first establish the basic facts before those facts can be integrated. This narrow focus on single facts is the starting point for the literature on meta-analysis.

Consider a theoretical question such as "Does job satisfaction increase organizational commitment?" Before we can answer such a question, we must answer the more mundane question: "Is there a correlation between satisfaction and commitment?" Such questions cannot be answered in any one empirical study. Few social scientists have the resources to do the large-sample studies required to obtain the necessary population statistics. Results must be pooled across studies to eliminate sampling error. Furthermore, the correlation between satisfaction and commitment might vary from one setting to the next. To check for this we must compare results across studies. That is, we must compare the population correlations in different settings. If there is variation across settings that is large enough to be theoretically important, then we must identify the moderator variables that produce this variation. In order to compare correlations across settings, we must correct these correlations for other artifacts such as measurement error or range variation. If the necessary information is given for each study, then error of measurement can be eliminated with the formula for correction for attenuation, and all results could be cast in terms of the same reference population or treatment strength using the range variation formula. Otherwise, these effects must be corrected for in the meta-analysis.

Consider error of measurement. Satisfaction can be measured in many ways. These different methods might differ in two ways: different methods may not measure exactly the same thing, or they may differ in the extent of random error in each method. Differences in random error can be assessed by differences in reliability coefficients. If the reliability of each measure is known in each study, then the effect of random error of measurement could be eliminated from each study by correcting the correlation or effect-size statistic for attenuation. If only the distribution or reliability coefficients across studies is known, then the effect of random error of measurement can be eliminated using special meta-analysis formulas.

Systematic differences between measures with the same name require examination of the construct validity of the different methods. If there are large systematic differences between measures, then these must be assessed in multimeasure studies using techniques such as confirmatory factor analysis or path analysis. These studies have replication of results within studies as well as across studies and require special treatment.

Range variation on the independent variable produces differences of an artifactual nature in correlations and in effect-size statistics. If the basic relationship between variables is the same across studies, then variation in the extent of variance on the independent variable will produce variation in the correlation with the dependent variable. The larger the variance on the independent variable, the higher the correlation. In experimental studies, range variation is produced by differences in the strength of the treatment. If the range size in each study is known (i.e., if standard deviations are published or if treatment strengths are measured), then all correlations or effect sizes could be corrected to some standard value. This would eliminate range variation across studies. If the distribution of range variation is known, then this effect can be eliminated using special meta-analysis formulas.

Meta-analysis begins with the set of all studies that an investigator has found that provide empirical evidence that bears on some particular fact such as the relationship between organizational commitment and job satisfaction. The key findings of each study are expressed in a common statistic such as the correlation between commitment and satisfaction or such as the d statistic, which measures the difference between experimental and control groups for the treatment of interest. Each such statistic can be examined across studies. The mean value of the statistic across studies is a good estimate of the mean population value across studies. However, the variance across studies is greatly inflated by sampling error. Thus the first task in meta-analysis is to correct the observed variance across studies to eliminate the effect of sampling error. Then the mean and variance of population values are corrected for the effect of error of measurement and range variation. This mean and standard deviation have thus been corrected for the three largest sources of artifactual variation across studies: sampling error, error of measurement, and range variation. The largest source of variation not corrected for is reporting error such as incorrect computations, typographical errors, failure to reverse score, and the like.

In many studies we have found no variance in results across studies once artifacts such as sampling error have been eliminated. In such cases the theorist is provided with a very straightforward fact to weave into the overall picture. For example, one way to obtain theoretical implications is to review all the reasons that have been cited as explanations for the nonexistent variation across studies. Most such explanations are based on more general theoretical considerations. Hence the disconfirmation of the explanation leads to disconfirmation of the more general propositions behind the explanation. For example, meta-analysis has shown that the correlation between cognitive ability factors and job performance does not vary across settings for a given job. This means that it is a waste of time for people in personnel research to do massive, detailed behavioristic job analyses to equate jobs with the same job description in different organizations.

If there is variation across studies, it may not be large enough to warrant an immediate search for moderator variables. For example, suppose that meta-analysis had shown the mean effect of interpersonal skills training on supervisor performance to be $\bar{\delta}$ = .50 with a standard deviation of .05. It would be wise for an employer to institute a program of training immediately rather than wait to find out which programs work best. On the other hand, if the mean effect were $\bar{\delta}$ = .10 with a standard deviation of .10, then the arbitrary choice of program might incur loss. There is a 16 percent chance that the program would be counterproductive, and another 34 percent chance that the program would cause a positive but nearly trivial improvement.

If there are large differences between studies, then moderator variables are usually not hard to find. For example, by the time the first meta-analysis was done on the effects of incentive on work performance, there were already interactive studies done showing that incentive only works if the worker is given specific feedback as to what aspects of performance are relevant to the rewarded outcome.

Meta-analysis provides a method for establishing the relevance of a potential moderator variable. The moderator variable is used to split the studies into subsets. Meta-analysis is then applied to each subset separately. Large mean differences should appear. If there are large differences in subset means, then there will be a corresponding reduction in within-subset variation across studies. Meta-analysis shows how much of that residual variation is due to artifacts.

The extent of variation is in part a question of the scope of the research review. If we start with all studies on psychotherapy, it is no surprise to find moderator effects. However, if we consider only studies using desensitization on snake phobias, then we might expect to find no differences. For meta-analysis, scope is an empirical question. If we have the resources for a wide scope, then meta-analysis can be used to assess the extent of scope. If meta-analysis shows only minor differences over a very wide set of studies, then we have found that many hypotheses are of only minor importance. If the wide-scope study shows large differences, then meta-analysis can be applied to subsets of studies with smaller scope. Meta-analysis then shows which aspects of scope are truly important and which are only thought to be important.

The general finding of meta-analytic studies is that differences across studies are much smaller than people believe them to be. This derives from the cumulative effect of sampling error; i.e., exposure to large but spurious differences in the observed results from small-sample studies.

A key point of consensus in meta-analysis is that restriction of scope should be topical rather than methodological. The worst reviews are those in which the author cites only "key" studies. First, reviews that selectively ignore studies with contrary findings may falsely suggest that there are no moderator variables. Second, even if there are no real variations across studies, there are spurious variations due to sampling error. Studies with particularly "sharp" findings are probably studies that capitalize on chance from the perspective of meta-analysis. In particular, consideration of only studies with statistically significant findings leads to great bias in the estimate of correlations or effect sizes.

Many authors justify selective reviews on the basis of the "methodological deficiencies" in the studies not considered. However, the assertion of "deficiency" is usually based on a theory that is itself not empirically tested. Two authors could select mutually exclusive sets of studies from the same literature on the basis of "methodological flaws." Meta-analysis provides an empirical procedure for the identification of methodological deficiencies if there are any. First, use general abstracting services to build a comprehensive set of studies. Second, identify those that are believed to be "defective." Third, apply meta-analysis to all studies. If there is no variation across studies, then there is no difference between the "defective" studies and the "competent" studies. Fourth, if there is variation across all studies, then that variation may or may not be explained by separate meta-analyses of the "defective" and "nondefective" studies.

It is our belief that most real methodological problems are captured by the rubrics "error of measurement" and "range variation." Error of measurement is universal, though some studies may have much poorer measurement than others. The solution to this is to *measure* the deficiency and correct for it rather than throw away data.

References

Baker, P. C. Combining tests of significance in cross validation. *Educational and Psychological Measurement,* 1952, 12, 300-306.

Bartlett, C. J., Bobko, P., Mosier, S. B., & Hannan, R. Testing for fairness with a moderated multiple regression strategy: An alternative to differential analysis. *Personnel Psychology,* 1978, 31, 233-241.

Boehm, V. R. Differential prediction: A methodological artifact? *Journal of Applied Psychology,* 1977, 62, 146-154.

Bradley, J. V. *Distribution free statistical tests.* Englewood Cliffs, NJ: Prentice-Hall, 1968.

Brozek, J., & Tiede, K. Reliable and questionable significance in a series of statistical tests. *Psychological Bulletin,* 1952, 49, 339-344.

Callender, J. C., & Osburn, H. G. Development and test of a new model for generalization of validity. *Journal of Applied Psychology,* 1980, 65, 543-558.

Campbell, D. T., & Stanley, J. C. *Experimental and quasi-experimental designs for research.* Chicago: Rand McNally, 1963.

Cattin, P. The estimation of the predictive power of a regression model. *Journal of Applied Psychology,* 1980, 65, 407-414.

Cooper, H. M., & Rosenthal, R. Statistical Versus Traditional Procedures for Summarizing Research Findings. *Psychological Bulletin,* 1980, 87, 442-449.

Cronbach, L. J. Coefficient alpha and the internal structure of tests. *Psychometrika,* 1951, 16, 297-334.

Eagly, A. H. Sex differences in influenceability. *Psychological Bulletin,* 1978, 85, 86-116.

Ghiselli, E. E. *The validity of occupational aptitude tests.* New York: John Wiley, 1966.

Glass, G. V Primary, secondary and meta-analysis of research. *Educational Researcher,* 1976, 5, 3-8.

Glass, G. V Integrating findings: The meta-analysis of research. *Review of Research in Education,* 1977, 5, 351-379.

Glass, G. V The wisdom of scientific inquiry on education. *Journal of research in science teaching,* 1972, 9, 3-18.

Glass, G. V, McGaw, B. & Smith, M. L. *Meta-analysis in social research.* Beverly Hills, CA: Sage, 1981.

Hall, J. A. Gender effects in decoding nonverbal cues. *Psychological Bulletin,* 1978, 85, 845-857.

Hedges, L. V. *Combining the results of experiments using different scales of measurement.* Center for Educational Research, Stanford University, 1980.

Hedges, L. V., & Olkin, I. Vote-counting methods in research synthesis. *Psychological Bulletin*, 1980, 88, 359-369.

Hunter, J. E. *Path analysis: Longitudinal studies and causal analysis in program evaluation.* Invited address presented at the 85th American Psychological Association Convention, San Francisco, August 28, 1977.

Hunter, J. E. *Cumulating results across studies: A critique of factor analysis, cannonical correlation, MANOVA, and statistical significance testing.* Invited address presented to the 86th Annual Convention of the American Psychological Association, New York, September 3, 1979.

Hunter, J. E. Factor analysis. In P. Monge (Ed.), *Multivariate techniques in human communication research.* New York: Academic Press, 1980.

Hunter, J. E., & Gerbing, D. W. Unidimensional measurement, second-order factor analysis, and causal models. In B. M. Staw & L. L. Cummings (Eds.), *Research in organizational behavior (Vol. 4).* Greenwich, CT: JAI, 1982.

Hunter, J. E., & Schmidt, F. L. Differential and single group validity of employment tests by race: A critical analysis of three recent studies. *Journal of Applied Psychology,* 1978, 63, 1-11.

Hunter, J. E., Schmidt, F. L., & Hunter, R. Differential validity of employment tests by race: A comprehensive review and analysis. *Psychological Bulletin*, 1979, 31, 215-232.

Jackson, G. B. *Methods for reviewing and integrating research in the social sciences.* Final Reports to the National Science Foundation for Grant #DIS 76-20398. Washington, DC: Social Research Group, George Washington University, April 1978. (NTIS No. PB283 747/AS)

Jackson, G. B. Methods for integrative reviews. *Review of Educational Research,* 1980, 50, 438-460.

Jones, L. V., & Fiske, D. W. Models for testing the significance of combined results. *Psychological Bulletin,* 1953, 50, 375-382.

Katzell, R. A., & Dyer, F. J. Differential validity revived. *Journal of Applied Psychology,* 1977, 62, 137-145.

King, L. M., Hunter, J. E., & Schmidt, F. L. Halo in a multidimensional forced choice performance evaluation scale. *Journal of Applied Psychology,* 1980, 65, 507-516.

Kulik, J. P., Kulik, C. C., & Cohen, P. A. A meta-analyses of outcome studies of Keller's personalized system of instruction. *American Psychologist,* 1979, 34, 307-318.

Lent, R. H., Aurbach, H. A., & Levin, L. S. Research design and validity assessment. *Personnel Psychology,* 1971, 24, 247-274. (a)

Lent, R. H., Aurbach, H. A., & Levin, L. S. Predictors, criteria, and significant results. *Personnel Psychology,* 1971, 24, 519-533. (b)

Levine, J. M., Kramer, G. G., & Levine, E. N. Effects of alcohol on human performance: An integration of research findings based on an abilities classification. *Journal of Applied Psychology,* 1975, 60, 285-293.

Levine, J. M., Romashko, T., & Fleishman, E. A. Evaluation of an abilities classification system for integration and generalizing human performance research findings: An application to vigilance tasks. *Journal of Applied Psychology,* 1973, 58, 149-157.

Light, R. J., & Smith, P. V. Accumulating evidence: Procedures for resolving contradictions among different research studies. *Harvard Educational Review,* 1971, 41, 429-471.

Mosier, C. I. On the reliability of a weighted composite. *Psychometrika,* 1943, 8, 161-168.

O'Connor, E. J., Wexley, K. N., & Alexander, R. A. Single group validity: Fact or fallacy? *Journal of Applied Psychology,* 1975, 60, 352-355.

Pearlman, K., Schmidt, F. L., & Hunter, J. E. Validity generalization results for tests used to predict job proficiency and training success in clerical occupations. *Journal of Applied Psychology* 1980, 65, 373-406.

Rosenthal, R. Combining results of independent studies. *Psychological Bulletin,* 1978, 85, 185-193.

Rosenthal, R. The "file drawer problem" and tolerance for null results. *Psychological Bulletin,* 1979, 86, 638-641.

Rosenthal, R., & Rubin, D. B. Interpersonal expectancy effects: The first 345 studies. *The Behavioral and Brain Sciences,* 1978, 3, 377-415.

Schmidt, F. L., Berner, J. G., & Hunter, J. E. Racial differences in validity of employment tests: Reality or illusion? *Journal of Applied Psychology,* 1973, 58, 5-9.

Schmidt, F. L., Gast-Rosenberg, I., & Hunter, J. E. Validity generalization: Results for computer programmers. *Journal of Applied Psychology,* 1980, 65, 643-661.

Schmidt, F. L. & Hunter, J. E. Development of a general solution to the problem of validity generalization. *Journal of Applied Psychology,* 1977, 62, 529-540.

Schmidt, F. L., & Hunter, J. E. Moderator research and the law of small numbers. *Personnel Psychology,* 1978, 31, 215-232.

Schmidt, F. L., Hunter, J. E., & Caplan, J. R. Validity generalization results for two occupations in the petroleum industry. *Journal of Applied Psychology,* 1981, 66, 261-273.

Schmidt, F. L., Hunter, J. E., & Pearlman, K. Task differences as moderators of aptitude test validity in selection: A red herring. *Journal of Applied Psychology,* 1981, 66, 166-185.

Schmidt, F. L., Hunter, J. E., Pearlman, K., & Shane, G. S. Further tests of the Schmidt-Hunter Bayesian validity generalization procedure. *Personnel Psychology,* 1979, 32, 257-281.

Schmidt, F. L., Hunter, J. E., & Urry, V. E. Statistical power in criterion-related validation studies. *Journal of Applied Psychology,* 1976, 61, 473-485.

Schmidt, F. L., Pearlman, K., & Hunter, J. E. The validity and fairness of employment and educational tests for Hispanic Americans: a review and analysis. *Personnel Psychology,* 1980, 33, 705-724.

Schwab, D. P., Olian-Gottlieb, J. D., & Heneman, H. G., III. Between subject's expectancy theory research: A statistical review of studies predicting effort and performance. *Psychological Bulletin,* 1979, 86, 139-147.

Smith, M. L., & Glass, G. V. Meta-analyses of psychotherapy outcome studies. *American Psychologist,* 1977, 32, 752-760.

Thorndike, R. L. The effect of the interval between test and retest on the constancy of the IQ. *Journal of Educational Psychology,* 1933, 25, 543-549.

Bibliography

I. METHODOLOGICAL ARTICLES

Baker, P. C. Combining tests of significance in cross validation. *Educational and Psychological Measurement,* 1952, 12, 300-306.

Borgatta, E. F., & Jackson, D. J. Aggregate data: An overview. *Sociological Methods & Research,* 1979, 7, 379-383.

Borgatta, E. F., & Jackson, D. J. *Aggregate data: Analysis and interpretation.* Beverly Hills, CA: 1980.

Brozek, J., & Tiede, K. Reliable and questionable significance in a series of statistical tests. *Psychological Bulletin,* 1952, 49, 339-344.

Bryant, F. B., & Wortman, P. M. Secondary analysis: The case for data archives. *American Psychologist,* 1978, 33, 381-387.

Burnstein, L. Assessing differences between grouped and individual-level regression coefficients: Alternative approaches. *Sociological Methods & Research,* 1978, 7, 5-28.

Callender, J. C., & Osburn, H. G. Development and test of a new model for generalization of validity. *Journal of Applied Psychology,* 1980, 65, 543-558.

Callender, J. C., Osburn, H. G., & Greener, J. M. *Small sample tests of two validity generalization models.* Paper presented at the Annual Convention of the American Psychological Association, New York, September 1979.

Cooper, H. M. Statistically combining independent studies: A meta-analysis of sex differences in conformity research. *Journal of Personality and Social Psychology,* 1979, 37, 131-146.

Cooper, H. M. *The literature review: Elevating its status to scientific inquiry.* Center for Research in Social Behavior, University of Missouri-Columbia, Technical Report No. 238, December 1980.

Cooper, H. M., & Rosenthal, R. Statistical versus traditional procedures for summarizing research findings. *Psychological Bulletin,* 1980, 87, 442-449.

Educational Research Service. Class size research: A critique of recent meta-analyses. *Phi Delta Kappan,* 1980, 239-241.

Eysenck, H. J. An exercise in mega-silliness. *American Psychologist,* 1978, 33, 517.

Feldman, K. A. Using the work of others: Some observations on reviewing and integrating. *Sociology of Education,* 1971, 44, 86-102.

Glass, G. V Primary, secondary and meta-analysis of research. *Educational Researcher,* 1976, 5, 3-8.

Glass, G. V Integrating findings: The meta-analysis of research. *Review of Research in Education,* 1977, 5, 351-379.

Glass, G. V Reply to Mansfield and Bussey. *Educational Researcher,* 1978, 7, 3.

Glass, G. V Policy for the unpredictable (uncertainty research and policy). *Educational Researcher,* 1979, 12-14.

Glass, G. V On criticism of our class size/student achievement research: No points conceded. *Phi Delta Kappan,* 1980, 242-244.

Glass, G. V, & Smith, M. L. Reply to Eysenck. *American Psychologist,* 1978, 33, 517-518.

Gallo, P. S. Meta-analysis—a mixed meta-phor. *American Psychologist,* 1978, 33, 515-517.

Hedges, L. V., & Olkin, I. Vote-counting methods in research synthesis. *Psychological Bulletin,* 1980, 88, 359-369.

Hunter, J. E. *Cumulating results across studies: A critique of factor analysis, cannonical correlation, MANOVA, and statistical significance testing.* Invited address presented to the 86th Annual Convention of the American Psychological Association, New York, September 3, 1979.

Hunter, J. E., & Schmidt, F. L. Differential and single group validity of employment tests by race: A critical analysis of three recent studies. *Journal of Applied Psychology,* 1978, 63, 1-11.

Jackson, G. B. *Methods for reviewing and integrating research in the social sciences.* Final Report to the National Science Foundation for Grant #DIS 76-20398. Washington, D.C.: Social Research Group, George Washington University, April 1978. (NTIS No. PB283 747/AS)

Jackson, G. B. Methods for integrative reviews. *Review of Educational Research,* 1980, 50, 438-460.

Jones, L. V., & Fiske, D. W. Models for testing the significance of combined results. *Psychological Bulletin,* 1953, 50, 375-382.

Light, R. J. Capitalizing on variation: How conflicting research findings can be helpful for policy. *Educational Researcher,* 1979, 8(9).

Light, R. J., & Smith, P. V. Accumulating evidence: Procedures for resolving contradictions among different research studies. *Harvard Educational Review,* 1971, 41, 429-471.

Mansfield, R. S., & Bussey, T. V. Meta-analysis of research: A rejoinder to Glass. *Educational Researcher,* 1977, 6, 3.

McGaw, B., & Glass, G. V *Choice of the metric for effect size in meta-analysis.* Unpublished paper, Laboratory of Educational Research, University of Colorado, n.d.

Pillemer, D. B., & Light, R. J. Synthesizing outcomes: How to use research evidence from many studies. *Harvard Educational Review,* 1980, 50, 176-195.

Presby, S. Overly broad categories obscure important differences between therapies. *American Psychologist,* 1978, 33, 514-515.

Rosenthal, R. *Experimenter effects in behavioral research.* New York: Irvington, 1976.

Rosenthal, R. Combining results of independent studies. *Psychological Bulletin,* 1978, 85, 185-193.

School Practice and Service Division Dissemination and Resources Group. *Report on Conference on Knowledge Synthesis Interpretation.* (Draft) National Institute of Education, Washington, D.C., July 11-12, 1977.

Smith, M. L., & Glass, G. V Meta-analysis of psychotherapy outcome studies. *American Psychologist,* 1977, 32, 752-760.

Taveggia, Thomas C. Resolving research controversy through empirical cumulation: Toward reliable sociological knowledge. *Sociological Methods & Research,* 1974, 2, 395-407.

Viana, M.A.G. Statistical methods for summarizing independent correlational results. *Journal of Educational Statistics,* 1980, 83-104.

Walberg, H. J., & Haertel, E. H. (Guest Editors). *Research integration: The state of the art.* Special Issue of *Evaluation in Education,* 1980, 4, 1-42.

Methodological articles in this special issue are:

Introduction

> Walberg, H. J., & Haertel, E. H. Research integration: Introduction and overview, 5-10.

Section I—Research Integration Methodology

> Light, R. J. Synthesis methods: Some judgment calls that must be made, pp. 13-17.
> Rosenthal, R. Combining probabilities and the file drawer problem, pp. 18-21.
> Smith, M. L. Publication bias and meta-analysis, pp. 22-24.
> Hedges, Larry V. Unbiased estimation of effect size, pp. 25-27.
> Barton, M. A. Two new uses of indicator variables in meta-analysis, pp. 28-30.
> Jacobs, J. A., & Critelli, J. W. Treatment-outcome interactions, pp. 31-32.
> Cooper, H. M., & Rosenthal, R. A comparison of statistical and traditional procedures for summarizing research, pp. 33-36.
> Cahen, L. S. Meta-analysis—A technique with promise and problems, pp. 37-42.

Ward, S. A. *Studies of knowledge synthesis issues and methods.* Washington, DC: National Institute of Education, n.d.

II. APPLICATIONS

The following references are to integrative analyses of various bodies of research literature.

Boss, F. *Class size revisited: Glass and Smith in perspective.* Unpublished paper, East Syracuse, Minoa Central Schools, February 1979.

Brown, S. H. Validity generalization and situational moderation in the life insurance industry. *Journal of Applied Psychology,* 1981, 66, 664-667.

Cahen, L. S., & Filby, N. N. The class size achievement issue: New evidence and a research plan. *Phi Delta Kappan,* 1979, 492-495, 538-539.

Carlberg, C. *Meta-analysis of special education treatment techniques.* Ph.D. dissertation, tion, University of Colorado, 1979.

Cooper, H. M. Statistically combining independent studies: A meta-analysis of sex differences in conformity research. *Journal of Personality and Social Psychology,* 1979, 37, 131-146.

Cooper, H. M., Burger, J. M., & Good, T. L. *Gender differences in the intellectual-achievement control beliefs of young children.* Unpublished paper, Center for Research in Social Behavior, University of Missouri, 1979.

Ferguson, P. *Meta-analysis of the effects of Transcendental Meditation on psychological outcomes.* Unpublished paper, University of Colorado, 1978.

Glass, G. V, Coulter, D., Hartley, S., Hearold, S., Stuart, K., Kalk, J., & Sherretz, L. *Teacher "indirectness" and pupil achievement: An integration of findings.* Boulder: University of Colorado, Laboratory of Educational Research, 1977.

Glass, G. V, & Smith, M. L. Meta-analysis of research on the relationship of class-size and achievement. *Evaluation and Policy Analysis,* 1979, 1, 2-15.

Hall, J. A. Gender effects in decoding nonverbal cues. *Psychological Bulletin,* 1978, 85, 845-857.

Hartley, S. S. *Meta-analyses of the effects of individually paced instruction in mathematics.* Ph.D. dissertation, University of Colorado, 1977.

Hearold, S. *Meta-analysis of the effects of television on social behavior.* Ph.D. dissertation, University of Colorado, 1978.

Hunter, J. E., Schmidt, F. L., & Hunter, R. Differential validity of employment tests by race: A review and analysis. *Psychological Bulletin,* 1979 86, 721-735. (Shows validity differences by race occur no more frequently than expected by chance and that validity magnitudes are similar for blacks and whites).

Johnson, D. W., Maruyama, R. J., & Nelson, D. Effects of cooperative, competitive, and individualistic goal structures on achievement: A meta-analysis. *Psychological Bulletin,* 1981, 89, 47-62.

Koslow, M. J., & White, A. L. *A meta-analysis of selected advance organizer research reports from 1960-1977.* Paper presented at the Annual Meeting of National Association for Research in Science Teaching, Atlanta, Ga., March 21-23, 1979.

Kulik, J. A., Cohen, P. A., & Ebeling, B. J. Effectiveness of programmed instruction in higher education: A meta-analysis of findings. *Educational Evaluation and Policy Analysis,* in press.

Kulik, J. A., Kulik, C. C., & Cohen, P. A. A meta-analyses of outcome studies of Keller's personalized system of instruction. *American Psychologist,* 1979, 34, 307-318.

Kulik, J. A., Kulik, C. C., & Cohen, P. A. Research on audio-tutorial instruction: A meta-analysis of comparative studies. *Research in Higher Education,* 1979, 11, 321-341.

Kulik, J. A., Kulik, C. C., & Cohen, P. A. Effectiveness of computer-based college teaching: A meta-analysis of findings. *Review of Educational Research,* 1980, 50, 525-544.

Ladas, H. Summarizing research: a case study. *Review of Educational Research,* 1980, 50, 597-624.

Linn, R. L., Harnisch, D. L., & Dunbar, S. B. Validity generalization and situational specificity: An analysis of the prediction of first year grades in law school. *Applied Psychological Measurement,* 1981, 5, 281-289.

Luitan, J., Ames, W., & Ackerson, G. A meta-analysis of the effects of advance organizers on learning and retention. *American Educational Research Journal,* in press.

Miller, T. L. *The effects of drug therapy on psychological disorders.* Ph.D. Dissertation, University of Colorado, 1977.

Mitchel, J. O. *Cooperative studies and validity generalization.* Unpublished paper, Life Insurance Marketing and Research Association, 1979.

Olweus, D. Stability of aggressive reaction patterns in males: A review. *Psychological Bulletin,* 1979, 86, 852-875.

Pflaum, S. W., Walberg, H. J., Karegianes, M. L., & Rasher, S. P. Reading instruction: A quantitative analysis. *Educational Researcher,* 1980 (July-August), 12-18.

Pearlman, K. *The validity of tests used to select clerical personnel: A comprehensive summary and evaluation* (Technical Study TS-79-1). Washington, DC: U.S. Office of Personnel Management, Personnel Research and Development Center, August 1979. (NTIS No. PB 80-102650)

Pearlman, K., Schmidt, F. L., & Hunter, J. E. Validity generalization results for tests used to predict job proficiency and training success in clerical occupations. *Journal of Applied Psychology,* 1980, 65, 373-406.

Rosenthal, R. *Experimenter effects in behavioral research.* New York: Irvington Publishers, 1976.

Rosenthal, R., & Rubin, D. B. Interpersonal expectancy effects: The first 345 studies. *The Behavioral and Brain Sciences,* 1978, 3, 377-415.

Schmidt, F. L., Gast-Rosenberg, I., & Hunter, J. E. Validity generalization: Results for computer programmers. *Journal of Applied Psychology,* 1980, 65, 643-661.

Schmidt, F. L., & Hunter, J. E. Development of a general solution to the problem of validity generalization. *Journal of Applied Psychology,* 1977, 62, 529-540.

Schmidt, F. L., Hunter, J. E., & Caplan, J. R. Validity generalization results for two occupations in the petroleum industry. Journal of Applied Psychology, 1981, 66, 261-273.

Schmidt, F. L., Hunter, J. E., & Pearlman, K. Task differences as moderators of aptitude test validity in selection: A red herring. *Journal of Applied Psychology,* 1981, 66, 166-185.

Schmidt, F. L., Hunter, J. E., Pearlman, K., & Shane, G. S. Further tests of the Schmidt-Hunter Bayesian validity generalization procedure. *Personnel Psychology,* 1979, 32, 257-281.

Smith, M. L. *Sex bias in counseling and psychotherapy.* Boulder: University of Colorado, Laboratory of Educational Research, October 1978.

Smith, M. L., & Glass, G. V Meta-analyses of psychotherapy outcome studies. *American Psychologist,* 1977, 32, 752-760.

Smith, M. L., & Glass, G. V *Class-size and its relationship to attitudes and instruction.* Unpublished paper, Laboratory of Educational Research, University of Colorado, Boulder, Colorado, July 1979.

Strube, M. J., & Garcia, J. E. *A meta-analytic investigation of Fiedler's contingency model of leadership effectiveness.* Unpublished paper, University of Utah, 1980.

Walberg, H. J., & Haertel, E. H. *Research integration: The state of the art.* Special issue of *Evaluation in Education,* 1980, 4, 1-42.

Applications articles in this special issue are:

Peterson, P. L. Open versus traditional classrooms, pp. 58-60.

Lorentz, J. L., & Coker, H. Teacher behavior, pp. 61-63.

Kulik, J. A., & Kulik, C. C. Individualized college teaching, pp. 64-70.

Section III—Individual differences and special effects

Hall, J. A. Gender difference in skill and sending and interpreting non-verbal emotional cues, pp. 71-72.

Cooper, H. M., Burger, J. M., & Good, T. L. Gender differences in learning control beliefs of young children, pp. 73-75.

Shakeshaft, C. & McNamara, J. F. Women in academic administration, pp. 76-78.

White, K. R. Socio-economic status and academic achievement, pp. 79-81.

Horan, P. F., & Lynn, D. D. Learning hierarchies research, pp. 82-83.

Dickson, W. P. Referential communication performance, pp. 84-85.

Stumpf, S. A. Evaluation bias in student ratings, pp. 86-87.

Kavale, K. Psycholinguistic training, pp. 88-90.

Kavale, K., & Carlberg, C. Regular versus special class placement for exceptional children, pp. 91-93.

Hearold, S. L. Television and social behavior, pp. 94-95.

Miller, T. I. Drug therapy for psychological disorders, pp. 96-97.

Lynn, D. D., & Donovan, J. M. Medical versus surgical treatment of coronary artery disease, pp. 98-99.

Section IV—Programmatic Research Integration

Haertel, G. D., & Walberg, H. J. Investigating an educational productivity model, pp. 103-104.

Uguroglu, M. E., & Walberg, H. J. Motivation, pp. 105-106.

Iverson, B. K., & Walberg, H. J. Home environment, pp. 107-108.

Williams, P. A., Haertel, G. D., & Walberg, H. J. Media, pp. 109-110.

Ide, J. C., Parkerson, J., Haertel, G. D., & Walberg, H. J. Peer influences, pp. 111-112.

Haertel, G. D., Walberg, H. J., & Haertel, E. H. Classroom socio-psychological environment, pp. 113-114.

Lysakowski, R. S., & Walberg, H. J. Classroom reinforcement, pp. 115-116.

Fredrick, W. C. Instructional time, pp. 117-118.

Schiller, D., Walberg, H. J., & Haertel, G. D. Quality of instruction, pp. 119-120.

Pflaum, S. W., Walberg, H. J., Karegianes, M., & Rasher, S. P. Methods of teaching reading, pp. 121-122.

Hersholt, C. W., & Walberg, H. J. Teacher effectiveness, pp. 123-124.

Kremer, B. K., Boulanger, F. D., Haertel, G. D., & Walberg, H. J. Science education research, pp. 125-129.

Ward, S. A. Studies of knowledge synthesis, pp. 130-133.

White, K. R. *The relationship between socio economic status and academic achievement.* Ph.D. Dissertation, University of Colorado, 1976.

About the Authors

JOHN E. HUNTER is Professor of Psychology and Mathematics at Michigan State University. His primary research work in recent years has concentrated on personnel selection, test fairness, test utility, and test validity. Dr. Hunter, with Frank Schmidt, was awarded the James McKeen Cattell Award of the American Psychological Association for work on validity generalization. His long-term research interests focus on math models, including work in psychometric theory and path analysis, attitudes and communications, attitude change, group dynamics, social network development, compliance-gaining strategies, leadership development, political behavior, and prejudice.

FRANK L. SCHMIDT is Research Psychologist at both the U.S. Office of Personnel Management and George Washington University and is a Fellow of the American Psychological Association. He received his Ph.D. in industrial/organizational psychology from Purdue University, and served previously on the faculty at Michigan State University. He has published numerous articles on personnel psychology, primarily with John Hunter. It was their research on the generalizability of emloyment test validity that led to the development of the meta-analysis methods presented in this book.

GREGG B. JACKSON is a freelance social science research consultant in Washington, D.C. His current research interests include social science research utilization, meta-analysis, program evaluation, job training, and interaction analysis. His most recent publications include "Methods for Integrative Reviews," *Evaluating the Impact of Policy Research Reports, How to Prepare Evaluative Guides to Job Training Programs,* and *Where to Get Job Training in the D.C. Area.*